Understanding The Gospels
As Ancient Jewish Literature

Jeffrey P. García

First published in 2018 by
CARTA Jerusalem

Copyright © 2018
Carta Jerusalem, Ltd.
11 Rivka Street, P.O.B. 2500,
Jerusalem 9102401, Israel
E-mail: carta@carta.co.il
www.carta-jerusalem.com

Great care has been taken to establish sources of illustrations. If inadvertently we omitted to do so, due credit will be given in the next edition.

All rights reserved. No part of this book may be reprinted or reproduced or utilized in any form or by any electronic, mechanical, or other means now known or hereafter invented, including photocopying and recording, or in any information storage or retrieval system, without prior permission in writing from the publisher.

ISBN: 978-965-220-896-5

Printed in the United States of America

TABLE OF CONTENTS

Introduction 5

Sources for Understanding the Gospels 6
    The Hebrew Bible 6
    Jewish Literature Outside of the Bible 6
    The Dead Sea Scrolls of Qumran 7
    Josephus 7
    Rabbinic Literature 8
    Targumim 8
    Philo of Alexandria 8

Geography of the Land of Israel in the Gospels 9

Jewish Political History in the Gospels 13

Jewish Life in the Gospels 15
    Languages of the First Century AD 15
    The Birth of Jesus and Jewish Home Life 16
    Jewish Clothing and the Gospels 16
    The Pharisees, Sadducees, and Jesus 17
    The Baptism and Ritual Immersion 18
    The Synagogue at Nazareth and the Sabbath 20
    Prayer 20
    Women in Jesus' Ministry 20
    A Pre–70 Passover Meal, but not a *Seder* 21
    Jerusalem's Temple 22
    Crucifixion and Death 24

Jewish Styles of Teaching in the Gospels 26
    Parables 26
    Halakhah (Jewish Law/Commandments) 27
    Jewish Styles of Biblical Interpretation 29

Charity, Deeds of Reciprocal Kindness, and the Image of God in the Gospels 33

The Gospels as the First Literary Witness to Jewish Practice 36
    Naming on the Eighth Day 36
    Abraham's Bosom 37
    The Reading of the *Haftarah* 37
    Preservation of Life (*pikuach nefesh*) 37
    Ritual Fringes (*tzitzit*) 38
    Attendance of Synagogue on the Sabbath 38
    Narration of Passover Pre–70 Meal 38
    Narration of Jewish Pilgrimage 38

Notes and References 39

LAND OF ISRAEL IN THE TIME OF JESUS

INTRODUCTION

In recent decades, scholars have made advances in shedding light on the Jewish backgrounds of the Gospels. This is largely the result of the so-called "Third Quest for the Historical Jesus," which distinguishes itself by attempts to place Jesus back into his ancient Jewish setting, although it is worth noting that three Jewish scholars—predating the Third Quest by one to three decades—were already examining Jesus' teachings in light of Jewish sources.[1] Yet, for all its success, the examination of Jewish "backgrounds" often relegate the Gospels to something other than the ancient Jewish culture where they originated. Of course, ancient Judaism did not develop in a vacuum. Judaism in the Second Temple period is vibrant, organic, and evolving. It is more than just the universality of one God and Torah—i.e., a common Judaism, if you will—but is influenced, to some degree, by the cultures that were present in the land of Israel (Persian, Hellenistic, Roman, etc.), which are most evident in the diverse linguistic landscape of the 1st century AD (Hebrew, Aramaic, and Greek).

Understanding the Gospels must begin with some important questions. From what cultural world do the Gospels emerge? How does understanding that ancient cultural landscape help us to understand the Gospels? What role do these texts play in being a witness, conserver, and representative part of that cultural world? Does Judaism simply play a background role, or does it have an integral place in the very texts that come to be defined as gospels? Of course, ascertaining these answers is complicated by a number of historical and textual considerations: (1) the traditions surrounding the Jesus movement were first passed on (performed) orally, and afterward, were written down; (2) the sources (Hebrew, Greek,

David Flusser (Courtesy of Jerusalem Perspective; photo David Harris).

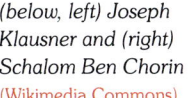

(below, left) Joseph Klausner and (right) Schalom Ben Chorin (Wikimedia Commons).

Albert Schweitzer, 1952. His The Quest for the Historical Jesus, *in 1906, was the first major work to coin the term Historical Jesus and review the work of other Jesus scholars. In his view, Jesus was primarily an apocalyptic figure* (Nobel Foundation, via Wikimedia Commons).

and perhaps Aramaic)—namely, texts, eyewitnesses, and/or performances—utilized, and attributed to four Evangelists, began to be compiled no later than 20–30 years after the crucifixion; and (3) the Gospel manuscripts as we have them now are more closely dated to the early 2nd century AD than the 1st century AD. Even with these historical twists and turns, however, it remains without argument that the Gospels collectively portray the Jesus movement as emerging from Second Temple Judaism.[2] Numerous studies have shown that they preserve already-known motifs, traditions, and language that predate the Gospels (e.g., the Dead Sea Scrolls) and bear some striking parallels to the earliest layers of Rabbinic thought (i.e., Tannaitic literature).[3] Moreover, the Gospels play a key role in Judaism as being both the first historical witness to Jewish practice that is only codified again in much later Jewish texts (even later Amoraic *midrashim*), attesting to the evolution of Judaism between the Second Temple period (ends AD 70) and the codification of oral traditions in the Mishnah and Tosefta (AD 200)—a period for which detailed sources are scarce.

Despite this reality, there remains a distinct separation between the fields of Second Temple Judaism and New Testament studies. Evidently, identifying the Gospels as "Jewish" seems to remain in flux, since they are often treated as outliers, or are of ancillary concern, in examinations of the ancient Jewish world. Yet, the Gospels, as we have them—despite the accretion of traditions (Roman, etc.) that come from early Christianity (2nd–3rd cent. AD) and the Evangelists' own particular styles—remain, at their core, Jewish texts. They are part of the corpora known as Greco-Roman Jewish literature and are not some radical offshoot. While it must not be ignored that some parts of the Gospels have been influenced by early Christianity's changing, although not yet separate relationship with the rest of Judaism, understanding how they function as sources of ancient Judaism is attainable. Therefore, the purpose of this work is not to recover the Jewish background of the Gospels, but to shed light on how they function as a source of ancient Jewish practice and culture and how that can help us to clarify some of the teachings attributed to Jesus by the Evangelists.

SECOND TEMPLE JUDAISM: Represents Judaism as it evolves from after the Babylonian Exile in 538 BC to the destruction of the Temple in AD 70.

TANNAITIC LITERATURE is a collection of texts and traditions, primarily halakhic (legal), and some aggadic (non-halakhic), that are thought to belong to the *Tannaim* (1st–3rd cent. AD). It includes the Mishnah, Tosefta, and *Halakhic Midrashim*.

AMORAIC MIDRASHIM: The *Amoraic Midrashim* are a collection of interpretations of the Torah that belong to the generation of rabbis after the *Tannaim* (i.e., sages who existed between the late 3rd–6th cent. AD), the earliest generation of rabbis. Many of the traditions associated with this generation also appear in the Jerusalem and Babylonian Talmuds (see below).

MISHNAH: The Mishnah is one of the earliest collections of interpretations of the Jewish law that were up to that time passed down orally. Sources state that Yehudah ha-Nasi (Judah the Prince) was responsible for writing them down in the Galilean city of Sepphoris in AD 200. The contents of the Mishnah are often associated with Rabbi Akiva and his school, although the actual composition of the Mishnah is far more complex.

TOSEFTA: The Tosefta is a supplement to the Mishnah, an addition to the initial collection of oral laws that are associated with the school of Rabbi Ishmael. Scholars have now noted that some of the traditions in the Tosefta pre-date those in the Mishnah and that its relationship as a supplement needs to be re-assessed.

SOURCES FOR UNDERSTANDING THE GOSPELS

Aerial view of El Araj, possible site of Bethsaida (photo Zachary Wong).

BIBLE: All evidence suggests that the canon of the Bible was still somewhat in flux during the Second Temple period, especially the "Writings" (e.g., Psalms). While certain communities appear to hold books outside of this collection as authoritative (e.g., *Jubilees* and *1 Enoch*), the frequent use of the books of Moses (Torah), Prophets (e.g., Isaiah, Jeremiah), and Psalms in related literature imply some degree of authoritativeness.

DEUTERONOMY: *deuteronomos* = second law.

1 AND 2 CHRONICLES: One of the more important aspects of Chronicles is how it interprets the rule of David in order to portray the king in a new light. Some of the more impressive examples are the omission of any reference to David's transgression with Bathsheba (2 Sam 11) and the insertion of Satan as having instigated David to complete the census of Israel (2 Sam 24:1–17/ 1 Chr 21).

EXTRA-BIBLICAL TEXTS: These are sometimes referred to as "post-biblical" (i.e., after the closing of the Hebrew Bible) or "intertestamental" (i.e., appearing between the Old and New Testament) literature. These are problematic categories because they are communal-specific (Jewish/Christian) and do not deal naturally with the literary complexities of how specific canons were formed or the dating of these works, some of which are known in their final form only in the early Christian period (3rd cent. AD). "Extra-biblical," while still suffering from some of this faulty categorization, is intended to identify literature that does not appear in either the OT or NT canons without getting stuck in the mire of dating, authority, etc.

Understanding the Gospels requires more than one discipline. The Gospels as texts are witnesses to a historically charged and culturally vibrant environment. In part, studies of these texts require a facility in ancient languages (e.g., Hebrew, Aramaic, and Greek) and an understanding of the geography of Roman Judaea, Samaria, the Galilee, Transjordan, and the Jaulan (Golan), as well as an examination of the archaeological innovations and excavations that have been made in the land of Israel since the late 19th and early 20th centuries. Continual excavations in Jerusalem and its environs, along with new digs in Magdala and El Araj (perhaps Bethsaida-Julias[4]) in the Galilee are revolutionizing what we know about life in the first century AD. These areas of language, geography, and archaeology, and their various complexities, are critical to examining the Gospels. In particular, textual sources are critical because they provide a written account of how Judaism evolves before and after the time of Jesus. They attest to the developing landscape of Jewish thought and shed light on the Gospels' place on it. What follows is a brief survey of these texts and their importance to gathering information about ancient Judaism.

The Hebrew Bible. It is clear that the Hebrew Bible, especially the Torah, certain Prophets, and Psalms were especially influential to the writers of the Gospels and the rest of the New Testament. The most quoted biblical books in the New Testament are the Psalms, Isaiah, and Deuteronomy, in that order. One finds that after the return from exile in 538 BC, the establishment and resurgence of an identity with Judah in the land of Israel caused the returnees to look back at those texts they returned with—e.g., Deuteronomy and Isaiah—and utilize them in this burgeoning reconnection with the land, their national identity, and their God.

Moreover, having been compiled over several hundred years and capturing literary traditions, some of which span a couple thousand years, the Hebrew Bible is also key because it shows how particular biblical texts were interpreted by later Judahite (associated with the southern kingdom of Judah) communities. For example, Deuteronomy, the second giving of the law, is largely a rewrite and interpretation of Exodus. So also, 1 and 2 Chronicles are works that are interpreting many of the accounts in the books of Samuel and Kings. Books such as 1 and 2 Chronicles, Daniel, and others, were composed after the exile (6th cent. BC) and, as a result, capture how these communities received their earlier sacred texts.

Jewish Literature Outside of the Bible. Already in the 3rd century BC, there is evidence of a growing number of extra-biblical texts. Some of them eventually became part of the Greek translation of Scriptures that came to be known as the Septuagint (LXX) in the 5th century AD. Some of these works were considered apocryphal—works of unknown authorship and of obscure origin—and are varyingly catalogued in collections known as the Apocrypha (i.e., hidden things). Defining these works as the Apocrypha is not an ancient category, however, and they likely circulated independently before being associated with the larger Greek translation of the Bible.

Beyond the Apocrypha, other extra-biblical works attest to the vibrancy of the ancient Jewish literary imagination. In regard to biblical interpretation, it was fairly common for ancient authors to write down their interpretations. Some of these works account for expanded versions of what were otherwise shorter biblical narratives. These terse fast-moving biblical narratives are often supplemented by the authors' interpretation, which can include adding or omitting details that do not appear in the original account. These evolving traditions also make their way into the New Testament. For example, 2 Timothy names Jannes and Jambres (2 Tim 3:8; see Acts 13:8) as the Egyptian priests who opposed Moses in Exodus (7:11), but these priests are not named in the book; they are anonymous. The book of Jude refers to the archangel Michael and devil contending over the body of Moses after his death—a tradition that is not attested in the Hebrew Bible.

This literary activity was not limited, however, to biblical interpretation, although the language, influence, and motifs that are prevalent in the Hebrew Bible saturate these corpora. Other extra-biblical texts bear evidence of a myriad of genres: apocalyptic, psalmic, prayers, and odes, rewritten and para-biblical literature, historical and philosophical treatises, testaments, etc. Many of these were composed pseudepigraphically, that is, writings that were falsely attributed to particular biblical figures. Some of these are compiled into modern collections called the Pseudepigrapha, which reflect Jewish works that were composed either before or during the time period depicted in the Gospels. Particular works, having originated in the early Jewish world, find their final forms after the destruction of the Temple (AD 70) but are still important for understanding the world of the Gospels (e.g., the *Testament of Abraham*).[5]

The Dead Sea Scrolls of Qumran. The next important collection that represents Jewish literary activity outside of the Bible are the Dead Sea Scrolls. In particular, are the nearly 1,000 scrolls discovered in 11 caves that scholars have connected primarily with the community that lived at Khirbet (Arab. "ruins") Qumran. Most of these documents were discovered between 1947 and 1956. Written

The War Scroll (Library of Congress; Matson Photo Service, American Colony).

mostly on parchment—with a small number on papyrus—the texts reflect the trilingual landscape of the 1st century AD. The majority are written in Hebrew, then Aramaic, and, finally, a small number of texts are written in Greek. Some of them (written all in Hebrew) were composed by the community, known as the *yaḥad*, that lived in and around the caves surrounding the site of Qumran from the end of the 2nd century BC to about AD 70. Not all were composed by the community, and many originate from elsewhere, perhaps even, outside of the land of Israel. Others originate from a time before the settlement at Qumran (e.g., Temple Scroll [11QT]) and reflect the thinking of the Qumran community as well as that of the Jewish world both in the land of Israel and those communities east of it. The Dead Sea Scrolls, in that sense, represent, as Frank Moore Cross referred to them, an ancient library.[6] Despite what a small number of scholars asserted early on, there are no New Testament texts or fragments extant among the collection.

Josephus. A former commander of the Galilee during the First Jewish Revolt against Rome (AD 66–73) turned Roman historian, Flavius Josephus (Jewish name: Yosef ben Matityahu) is responsible for providing us with the most detailed history of the Second Temple period. Among his works are *Jewish War*, a detailing of Jewish history between the period of the Hasmoneans and end of the first revolt; *Jewish Antiquities*, another accounting of history from the beginning of Genesis through the first Jewish revolt. Both are important historiographical resources for the first century. *Antiquities* is distinguished partly from *War* with its numerous interpretations and expansions of biblical narratives that were also around in the New Testament period. His final two works *Life* and *Against Apion* are a biographical account of the historian's life and an ancient apologetic work arguing for the antiquity of Judaism against pagan criticism from Apion, and Manetho, respectively. As a Greco-Roman writer, Josephus' works, which are sources of Jewish history and thought, are also

> **APOCRYPHA:** 1–2 Esdras, Tobit, Judith, Additions to Esther, Wisdom of Solomon, Sirach (Ben Sira), Additions to Daniel—Prayers of Azariah, Susanna, Bel and the Dragon, Prayer of Manasseh, 1–4 Maccabees, Psalm 151.

> **PSEUDEPIGRAPHA:** (1) A *pseudo graphe* is a text whose author is unknown or masked under the name of another person, usually a prominent biblical figure (e.g., 1 Enoch); (2) modern collections of Jewish literature that were not canonized, generally not part of the so-called Apocrypha, and are extra-biblical (e.g., Testament of the Twelve Patriarchs; The Life of Adam and Eve).

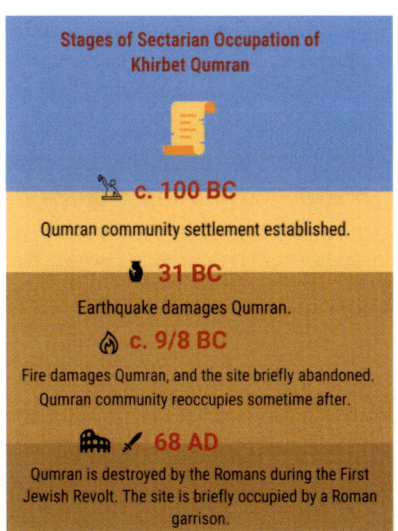

Stages of occupation at Kh. Qumran, according to Jodi Magness (in *The Archaeology of the Holy Land*; Cambridge UP, 2012, 112).

Artist's rendition of Josephus (after engraving appearing in William Whiston's translation of his works).

Ruins of Khirbet Qumran, looking southeast (photo Samuel Magal).

YEHUDAH HA-NASI (THE PRINCE): The chief redactor and editor of the Mishnah, which was compiled in the Galilean town of Sepphoris.

TRANSMISSION LEGEND: "Moses received the Torah at Sinai and handed it on to Joshua, Joshua to elders, and elders to prophets, and prophets handed it on to the men of the great assembly…and on to Simon the Righteous" [*m. Avot* 1:1].

LITERATURE OF THE TANNAIM: Mishnah, Tosefta, Halakhic Midrashim—*Sifre* to Deuteronomy, *Sifra* to Leviticus (*Torat Cohanim*), *Mekhilta de-Rabbi Ishmael*, and, perhaps, *Mekhilta de-Shimon bar Yohai*, *Sifre Zutta*.

TARGUM TEXTS: Onkelos, Neophyti, Pseudo-Yonatan, and Fragments.

heavily influenced by the Roman world that he lived in while writing them.

Rabbinic Literature. Scholars are divided as to the value and use of rabbinic literature for understanding the Gospels. The reason for this is that the earliest texts of the rabbis were compiled in the 3rd century AD by Yehudah ha-Nasi (Judah the Prince) after the Gospels and the New Testament were completed. Indeed, this is more than two hundred years from the time depicted by the Evangelists. Yet, rabbinic literature is purported to be a collection of oral traditions that existed from the time of Sinai (*m. Avot* 1:1).

While this tradition of succession is mostly legendary, there is evidence of an oral tradition—an oral law—that existed prior to their writing. Numerous legal and non-legal traditions that appear in the earliest layers of rabbinic literature also closely parallel Second Temple literary sources, including the New Testament.[7] Yet, there are also aggadic (non-legal) *midrashim* (e.g., *Genesis* and *Leviticus Rabbah*) and *baraitot* (Tannaitic sayings, originally oral, that are not recorded in the Mishnah), which while dated to later than the Tannaitic collections, also share some surprising parallels. Even as rabbinic literature evolves into the so-called "sea" of scholarly debate, parallels to the New Testament can be found in the 5th century AD Jerusalem Talmud and the 8th century AD Babylonian Talmud, although the similarities in thought in the latter are not as prevalent. Undoubtedly, when utilized critically, the literature of the Sages—rabbinic literature—especially the earliest texts, namely, those of the Tannaim, can be fruitful to understanding early Judaism, as well as Jesus' ministry and teachings.[8]

Targumim. The *Targumim* are not merely Aramaic translations of the Hebrew Bible. They originate outside of the land of Israel and contain numerous interpretive expansions and paraphrases that move beyond what one would call "translation"—that is, the expression of the meaning of a text from one language to a target language. Some of these interpretations originate in early Judaism and are attested in the Gospels, as well in the Dead Sea Scrolls and other extra-biblical texts. There are Aramaic translations of biblical texts (e.g., 11QtJob)—mostly in fragments—from the early Roman period, but it is likely that these were intended to function as actual translations rather than the interpretations or commentaries that are preserved in the *Targumim* referenced here. For all intents and purposes, despite having some connection to the 1st century BC and AD texts, the *Targumim*, as a whole, are a post-Second Temple period phenomenon.

Philo of Alexandria. The prolific Jewish philosopher of Alexandria is an important source for early Judaism. He flourished between the first century BC and AD. Philo Judaeus is known for allegorizing biblical narratives and seeing the distinctly Jewish texts through Hellenistic philosophical lenses. His works also provide a window into Jewish practice and are a witness to the diversity of Jewish thought outside of the land of Israel.

Philo of Alexandria (by André Thévet, 1584).

GEOGRAPHY OF THE LAND OF ISRAEL IN THE GOSPELS

The Gospels are deeply connected to the land of Israel. This is indicated by the numerous geographical references. Early in Matthew and Luke, the reader is introduced to two areas of particular interest, Judea and Galilee, via Bethlehem (Matt 2:1; Luke 2:4) and Nazareth (Matt 2:23; Luke 1:26; Mark 1:9), respectively. Both were small Jewish villages in the first century of which Bethlehem is the only one to receive mention in Second Temple sources outside of the Gospels (*Ant.* 6–8).[9] The two cities' continued existence into the modern period—both being very large Arab cities—have prevented extensive archaeological work, although there is evidence of first-century Jewish life.

Clay seal (bulla)—middle line reads bat lechem, *i.e., Bethlehem* (courtesy Israel Antiquities Authority).

vergence of four streams (headwaters)—the Dan, Banias, Hatsbani, and the Iyyon. R. Steven Notley has already shown that reading the Gospels in light of ancient sources indicates that John's baptismal events occur in its northern stretches in the so-called "wilderness" (*eremos*: ἔρημος [Heb. *midbar*: מִדְבָּר]; i.e., pastoral, deserted lands) of Bethsaida (Mark 6:32; Luke 9:10), rather than south of the lake.[10]

The Gospels' geographical references before and after the baptism show their awareness of the Jordan River as a geographical-political boundary between the Galilee and Gaulanitis, east of the Galilee. First, Matthew tells us that Jesus comes "from the Galilee" (*apo tes galilaias*: ἀπὸ τῆς Γαλιλαίας) to the area of the Jordan to John (Matt 3:13), which suggests that the area of John's baptisms, in this occasion, is no longer technically in the Galilee. Second, Luke tells us that Jesus returns "into the Galilee" (*eis ten galilailan*: εἰς τὴν Γαλιλαίαν) after his temptation in the "wilderness" (Luke 4:14). Third, John's baptisms are said to take place "beyond the Jordan" (*peran tou iordanou*: πέραν τοῦ Ἰορδάνου; Matt 4:25; John 1:28), which means east of the Jordan in what was a new polity under the control of Herod Philip (tetrarch), not Herod Antipas (tetrarch) who controlled the Galilee (see more on this below).

The Gospels depict Jesus' ministry as originating on the northwestern shores of the lake of Galilee. Derived from the Hebrew *gll* ("cylinder" or "district"), *Galilee* is the northernmost region of the land of Israel's central mountain range. To the west of Galilee is the northern stretch of the coastal plain and to the east lie the Jordan River Valley and the lake of Galilee. Roman sources indicate that the area was divided between Upper and Lower Galilee. The lower Galilee, in particular, consisted of a number of Jewish villages on the western side of the lake. Archaeology suggests that smaller towns and villages

Remains of a 1st-century house from Nazareth (photo Assaf Peretz; courtesy Israel Antiquities Authority).

The readers of Matthew and Luke are also introduced to the land of Israel's major waterway, the Jordan River, through John the Baptist's ministry:

> *In those days came John the Baptist, preaching in the wilderness of Judea, "Repent, for the kingdom of heaven is at hand." For this is he who was spoken of by the prophet Isaiah when he said, "The voice of one crying in the wilderness: Prepare the way of the Lord, make his paths straight." Now, John wore a garment of camel's hair, and a leather girdle around his waist; and his food was locusts and wild honey. Then went out to him Jerusalem and all Judea and all the region about the Jordan, and they were baptized by him in the river Jordan, confessing their sins.*
>
> (Matt 3:1–6)

While traditions of where John baptized have developed primarily around the river south of the lake of Galilee (a.k.a. Sea of Galilee) where the Jordan exits and continues down to the Dead Sea, most readers are unaware that technically the river begins north of the lake and meanders from north to south for 251 km (156 mi.) beginning at the con-

GALILEE IN THE FIRST CENTURY AD

(top) The Arbel Pass, looking northeast into the Galilee (photo Maureen Farrell García).

(above) Remains of Roman theater built by Herod Antipas in Tiberias (photo Jeffrey P. García).

Lupinus Legumes plants were used by Rabbi Shimon Bar Yohai to purify Tiberias (photo Zachi Evenor, via Wikimedia Commons).

PURIFICATION OF TIBERIAS: Rabbinic tradition credits R. Shimon bar Yohai with the purification of Tiberias at the beginning of the 2nd century AD. Varying accounts agree that Rabbi Shimon planted Lupine legumes and, depending on the account, whether they took root and grew or did not, the Sage would know where the graves were and could have the remains reburied elsewhere and purify the tombs.

(e.g., Nazareth) maintained a more defined Jewish identity, especially in the eastern lower Galilee. Larger cities like Sepphoris, the capital of the Galilee in Jesus' day, and, even, Tiberias, exhibited a mixture of elements that were both distinctly Jewish (e.g., ritual immersion baths) and predominantly Roman (e.g., theaters).

Matthew's "Sermon on the Mount" (Matt 5–7) and Luke's "Sermon on the Plain" (Luke 6:17–49) depict the two topographical markers that identify the area of the Galilee which sits nearly 700 feet (213 m) below sea level. Matthew states, "Seeing the crowds, he went up on the mountain (*anebes eis to opos*: ἀνέβη εἰς τὸ ὄρος), and when he sat down, his disciples came to him" (Matt 5:1). Except for two major plains around the lake, one on the western side of the lake of Galilee, known as Gennesaret (Matt 14:34)—a Greek form of the Hebrew "Genneisar" (גְּנֵיסָר; *m. Maas.* 3:7) or Gennesar—and another on the northeastern side of the lake, known as the "wilderness (or 'deserted place') of a town called Bethsaida" (*topon eremon poleos kaloumenes bethsaida*: τόπον ἔρημον πόλεως καλουμένης Βηθσαϊδά; Luke 9:10), the lake is surrounded by rolling high hills. Either of these plains fit the geographical reference in Luke 6:17: "And he came down with them and stood on a level plain (*epi topou pedinou*: ἐπὶ τόπου πεδινοῦ), with a great crowd of his disciples."

While Matthew and Luke seem to place the same event in different geographical locations, here is not the place to argue which Gospel correctly captures the original setting of the story. Suffice it to say that both Gospels present a collection of Jesus' teachings that occurred at various points during his ministry, which suggests that "plain" and "mount" are just generic geographic locations which the Evangelists employed to capture these Galilean teachings.

Jesus' visit to the synagogue of Nazareth (Luke 4:16–30) and in the village of Cana (John 2:1–11) imply his presence in the fertile plain of Gennesar. It is clear in Luke that the community in the synagogue of Nazareth was already familiar with the miracles that happened in Capernaum (Luke 4:23). This is not surprising since the three communities were closely connected geographically. One of the easier routes from Capernaum to Cana and Nazareth would have been to move south along the western side of the lake through the plain of Gennesar and perhaps at Magdala, which lies at the foot of Mount Arbel, work westward through the valley between Mount Arbel and Nitai. This route would also allow Jesus to avoid Tiberias, a city built by Herod Antipas that is not mentioned in the Synoptic Gospels (but see John 6:1, 6:23; 21:1), perhaps, because it was built over a cemetery so that the city would render Jewish inhabitants and visitors ritually unclean.

FROM CAPERNAUM TO NAZARETH

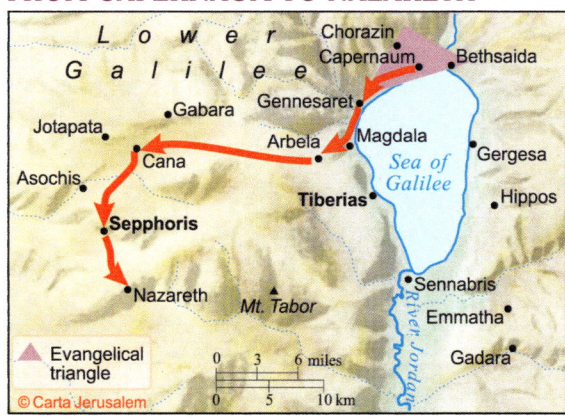

The majority of Jesus' ministry in the Gospels is depicted as being centered in and around three villages, Capernaum, Chorazin, and Bethsaida (cf. Matt 4:13, 11:21; Mark 6:45; Luke 10:13; John 1:44), although Jesus' travels south from the Galilee into Jerusalem and other locations allow his message to move beyond its Galilean confines. The Gospels tell us that Jesus went and taught in the synagogues of Galilee (Matt 4:23, 9:35; Mark 1:39; Luke 4:15). The discovery of a 1st century AD synagogue at Magdala, on the western side of the lake, is another indication that his ministry in the Galilee took him south of Capernaum into the area of Gennesar. He is also depicted as going to the eastern side of the lake in the pericope of the Gerasene (modern-day Jerash)/Gadarene (Gadara) demoniac (Matt 8:28–34; Mark 5:1–20; Luke 8:26–39). This account, which New Testament manuscript evidence indicates occurred at Gergesa (Kursi), on the eastern side of the lake—a better-fitting location for the geographical context of

Magdala: remains of the 1st-century synagogue (photo Jeffrey P. García).

(above) Front and side views of the ornately decorated stone, from the synagogue remains at Magdala (photos Jeffrey P. García).

(below) Wall fresco from the 1st-century synagogue at Magdala (photo Maureen Farrell García).

the Gospel stories—depicts the presence of pigs. It is notable that Gergesa (Kursi) sits near the outlet of Wadi es–Samak—a mostly dry riverbed that meanders west through the Golan Heights and into the lake of Galilee. Archaeological and historical sources have confirmed a predominantly Gentile presence south of Wadi es–Samak (see Hippos/Sussita). The presence of swine does not necessarily suggest a Gentile setting, since in Judaism it is forbidden to eat pork, but pigs are allowed to be used in other ways (*m. Kil.* 8:6).[11] North of the wadi as one works around the lake north and west through the Bethsaida (Buteiha) valley, Chorazin, Capernaum, and Gennesar valley, there is strong Jewish presence especially in smaller villages. Mordechai Aviam notes that sites closest to the lake along its northern and northwestern stretches and the lower Galilee west of the lake, but just east of the Mediterranean, maintained this identity.[12] The idea that the Galilee of Jesus was either heavily Hellenized—related to the so-called "Galilee of the Gentiles" (Matt 4:15)—and that the type of Judaism that developed there paled

AROUND THE LAKE

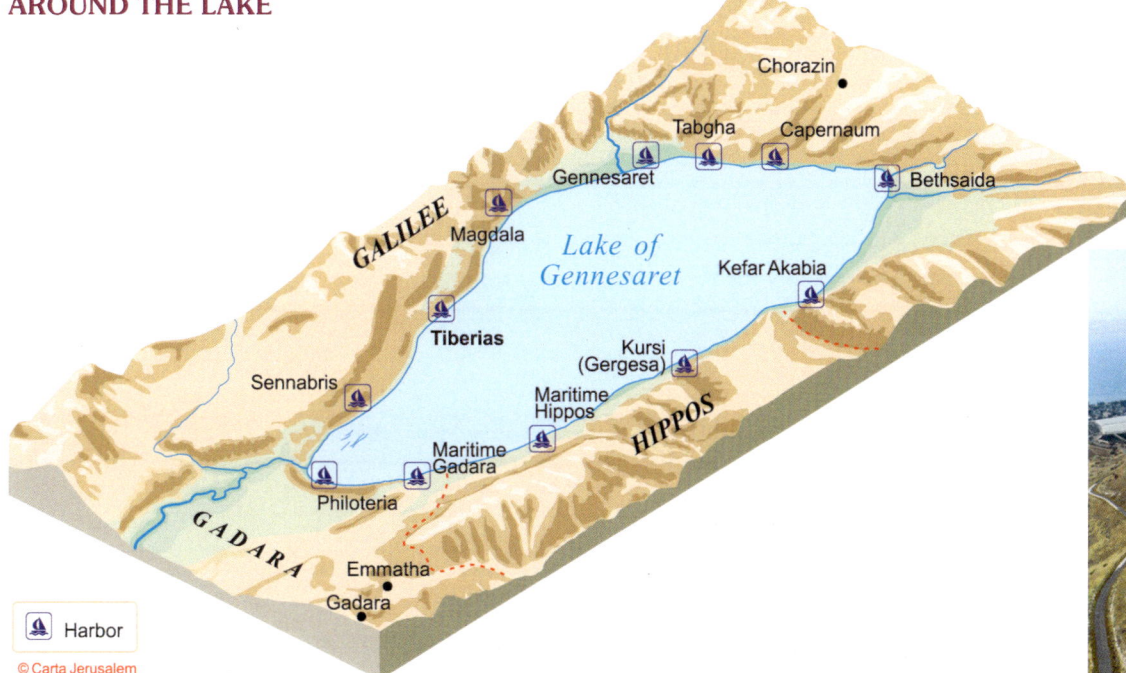

Aerial view of Hippos/Sussita, looking west (photo Michael Eisenberg, via Wikimedia Commons).

Second Temple period remains at Sepphoris (photo Maureen Farrell García).

Mona Lisa of the Galilee; 4th-century mosaic from Sepphoris (photo Maureen Farrell García).

The open cave in Caesarea Philippi (Paneas/Banias) where Pan was once worshipped (via Wikimedia Commons).

in substance, piety, and value when compared to that of Judea in the south should now be summarily dismissed.[13] As mentioned earlier, larger cities like Tiberias and Sepphoris were heavily influenced by Greco-Roman culture. Tiberias was ritually unclean until the 2nd century AD. Both cities would have had a Jewish presence, as well. Although, more pious Jews may have avoided visiting Tiberias or living in Sepphoris, returning especially to Sepphoris for work.

Mark and Matthew refer to Jesus being in the area (or villages; Mark 8:27) of Caesarea Philippi (modern-day Banias), but not in the city itself. This city would have been in Gaulanitis (modern-day Golan Heights) and the religious practice of worshipping Pan there (so, Paneas=Banias)—the god of nature and companion of the nymphs—might have caused Jesus and his followers to avoid entry. Mark's reference to "villages" (*tas komas*: τὰς κώμας) may suggest smaller settlements of Jews where Jesus and his followers would have found a more comfortable socio-religious setting. It is in this area that Jesus asked his disciples the well-known question, "Who do you say that I am?" (Matt 16:15; Mark 8:29; Luke 9:20). As a result of reference to the city, scholars have often associated Jesus' reference of the "gates of hell" with Pan's temple in Caesarea Philipi. The problems with this persisting suggestion are countless, including that none of the Gospels place Jesus inside the city. Indeed, nowhere—not even the Gospels—is the temple to Pan associated with a gate to the underworld as later Roman tradition speculated about other locales (e.g., Lacus Curtius by Livy the Historian).

Jewish communities in the Galilee also maintained a strong connection with Judea and Jerusalem, the city of the Great King (Matt 5:35; cf. Ps 48:2). There were three feast days that Galileans—and Jewish people from around the Mediterranean—would make pilgrimages to observe these holy days in Jerusalem: Passover (*pesach*), Feast of Weeks (*shavuot*; Pentecost), and Feast of Tabernacles (*sukkot*). Early on in Jesus' life, Luke depicts his family as pilgrims visiting Jerusalem during the Passover (Luke 2) and notes that they went "every year" (*kat etos*: κατ᾽ ἔτος), suggesting his family's heightened sense of piety. In fact, Jesus himself is depicted as a pilgrim on his final week of life, which also fell on Passover. The Gospels' depiction of Jesus', his family's, and followers' connection with Jerusalem is not unique to the Gospels but reflects the continual relationship between the Galilee and Jerusalem and Judea.

John depicts Jesus traveling through Samaria (4:9; cf. Luke 10:33), although tense relations between Jews and Samaritans may have caused Jesus to avoid passing through the area as he made his way south to Jerusalem. Avoiding Samaria is implied by Jesus' route from Jericho to Jerusalem (Matt 21:1; Mark 11:1; Luke 19:29). Getting to Jericho required travelling from the Galilee through the Jordan rift valley completely bypassing the heartland of Samaria (see Matt 21:1, Mark 11:1, Luke 19:29).

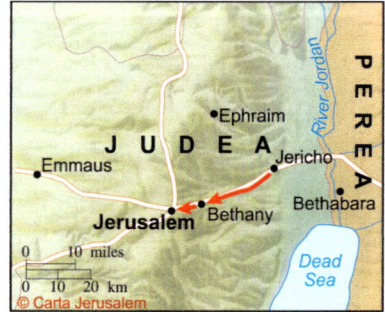

From Jericho to Jerusalem.

Additionally, the important Phoenician port cities of Tyre and Sidon are also referenced in the Gospels as places from where people come to seek healing from Jesus (Luke 6:17). After the resurrection, Luke speaks of the village named Emmaus (*komen…he onoma emmaous*: κώμην…ᾗ ὄνομα Ἐμμαοῦς; Luke 24:13), an important city in the Shephelah that was on the road from Jerusalem to Jaffa (see also 1 Macc 3:40, 57, 59; 4:3; 9:50).

Remains of the Roman road leading from Jerusalem to Emmaus (photo R. Steven Notley).

JEWISH POLITICAL HISTORY IN THE GOSPELS

Throughout the Gospels, the land of Israel is correctly depicted under the authority of the Roman Empire (cf. Luke 2:2). This political reality begins with General Pompey's siege of Jerusalem in 63 BC. By the time one opens the Gospels, there is no longer a Roman Senate and Rome has transitioned into an Empire. The first emperor, Augustus Ceasar, is already in power and he is succeeded in AD 14 by Tiberius, his adopted son.

Matthew and Luke,[14] however, are not initially concerned with the power of Rome as they are with letting the reader know that Herod the Great (73–4 BC) is "king" (*basileos*: βασιλέως) over the land of Israel (Luke 1:5; Matt 2:1). Under the influence of Mark Antony, the Roman Senate named Herod "King of Judaea" in 37 BC (*War* 1:282–285). The portrait painted of Herod in historical sources is one of a paranoid, power-hungry client king, who was deeply loyal to Rome, especially as it assured his continuing authority over the land. This characteristic of Herod the Great is on full display in Matthew 2 when Herod calls the *magi* in order to find where Jesus, the "king of the Jews" (Matt 2:2), had been born. Herod was disingenuous to state that he desired to worship the child. He is incensed after the *magi* do not return, and sends men to kill all males two years old and younger (Matt 2:16–17). Herod's paranoidal tendencies do not begin there as he is also responsible for killing his Hasmonean wife, Mariamne, and their two sons, Alexander and Aristobulus (see *War* 1:442–444, 550–551; also *Ant.* 17:44). He is, however, survived by his many building projects, all of which have made it through the passage of time in either monumental ruins or from being reused.

After Herod's death in 4 BC, his kingdom is divided among his three sons. Often they are referred to in the Gospels as "Herod" without their own distinguishing names (Matt 14:1; Mark 6:6; Luke 3:9). Herod Archelaus, ethnarch in control of Samaria, Judea, and Idumea (Edom, and Herod the Great's homeland) is referenced as ruling over Judea in Matthew 2:22. "Judea" here refers geographically to the portion of land between Samaria and Idumea. With their return to the land of Israel from Egypt (Matt 2:23)—after Herod the Great's death—Joseph and Mary avoided Archelaus' territory and withdrew into Galilee, which was under the control of Antipas.[15] Archelaus was noted for his cruelty—far surpassing his father—and his ardent desire to be named "king" over his brothers. His political ploy to regain his father's former authority was contested by a group of Jewish and Samaritan leaders who he had previously chosen to deal with barbarously.[16] Some suggest that Jesus' "Parable of the Pounds" (Luke 19:12–27) is partly an allusion to this event. As a result of this, Archelaus was deposed by Augustus Caesar and exiled to Vienna of Gaul in AD 6 (*War* 2:111). After his exile, Judea officially became a Roman province. The imposition of direct Roman rule in Judea brought with it a census, which in Luke happens under [Publius Sulpicius] Quirinius, governor of Syria (Luke 2:2; AD 10–12). Marc Turnage has already noted Luke's use of this event to literarily establish Roman authority over the land of Israel.[17] From that point, Rome was ever present,

Bust of Pompey (photo Alphanidon, via Wikimedia Commons).

Some of Herod's building projects (clockwise from below):

Western Wall of the Temple Mount (lower courses are Herodian stone) (photo Maureen Farrell García).

Cave of the Patriarchs at Hebron (photo Ricardo Tulio Gandelman, via Wikimedia Commons).

Aerial view of the remains at Masada, looking southeast (photo Samuel Magal).

THE DIVISION OF HEROD'S KINGDOM

Pilate Stone from Caesarea, now on display at the Israel Museum (photo Jeffrey P. García).
Inscription reads:
[   ]S TIBERIEUM
[...PONTI]US PILATUS
[...PRAEF]ECTUS IUDA[EA]E

[...]s Tiberium
[...Ponti]us Pilate
[...prefect of Jud[ae]a

(from *Greatness Grace & Glory: Carta's Atlas of Biblical Biography* / Paul H. Wright; © Carta Jerusalem)

learned that he belonged to Herod's jurisdiction (*ek tes exousias*: ἐκ τῆς ἐξουσίας), he sent him over to Herod, who was himself in Jerusalem at that time." Herod Philip, the third son to inherit a portion of Herod the Great's land, was a tetrarch in control of Batanea (or Bashan), Trachonitis, Auranitis, Gaulanitis, Paneas (Baneas[18]) and the Ulatha region.[19] He is referenced with Jesus' passing through the region of Caesarea Philippi (see above) and in Mark where Herod Antipas is said to have seized the Baptist because he openly spoke against Antipas' marriage to his brother Philip's wife, Herodias (Mark 6:17).

Luke, while being particularly precise with the Jewish political reality of the land of Israel, is also so in defining the religious leadership of the day.[20]

> *In the fifteenth year of the reign of Tiberius Caesar, Pontius Pilate being governor of Judea, and Herod being tetrarch of Galilee, and his brother Philip tetrarch of the region of Ituraea and Trachonitis, and Lysanias tetrarch of Abilene, in the high-priesthood of Annas and Caiaphas....*
>
> (Luke 3:1–2)

Along with listing Roman authority, the Evangelist includes the high priesthood of Annas and Caiaphas. Indeed, in the Second Temple period politics and religion were not separate spheres. While the high priest and priesthood played an important role in Jewish life in the land of Israel (see below), there appears to be a distinct relationship between the priestly elite, especially Caiaphas—son-in-law to Annas—and Pilate. During Jesus' last week of life, he is described by Luke as coming before Caiaphas and the elite of Jerusalem, Pilate, Herod Antipas, and Pilate once again (Luke 22:66–23:25), *not* the entire Sanhedrin. Pilate's and Caiaphas' allegiance is implied by the fact that the latter's tenure as high priest is the longest in the house of Annas (AD 18–36), and that both Pilate—removed from his position by Lucius Vitellius (*Ant*. 18:88–89)—and Caiaphas were deposed in the same year (AD 36/37).[21]

specifically in Judea, through a series of procurators and prefects. The most well known prefect, who is also responsible for Jesus' death, is Pontius Pilate.

After his father's death, Herod Antipas was named tetrarch in control of the Galilee and Perea in the Transjordan. Antipas, who is responsible for John the Baptist's imprisonment and death (Matt 14:3; Mark 14:10), is also referenced in the Passion accounts (Luke 23:11). Luke's Gospel is the only one to depict this political reality. In fact, when Pilate sends Jesus to Antipas, Pilate states: "And when he

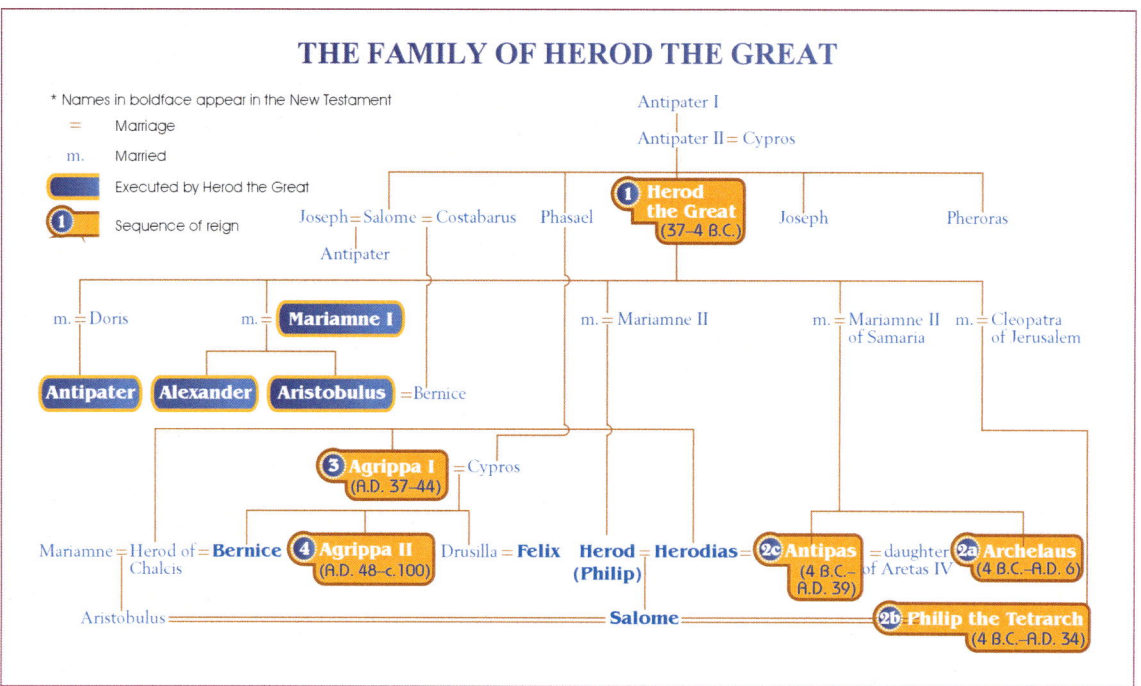

JEWISH LIFE IN THE GOSPELS

Judaism, which is primarily the post-exilic (late 6th century BC) evolution of a pre-exilic Judahite identity, experiences several formative moments during and after the Babylonian exile. Among many other examples were noticeable Persian influences that found their way into the Hebrew language, as well as revamped celestial (e.g., angels and demons) and dualistic conceptions of the world. With the advent of Hellenism into the east in 333/2 BC with Alexander the Great, Judaism was irrevocably changed in both its incorporation and fight against it. In fact, the complex forces that shaped Judaism between the fourth and first century BC would be foundational to the type of Judaism observed by Jesus and his disciples. As one opens the Gospels, Judaism is especially far removed from the world of the Israelites, and due to various revolts, a small period of Jewish autonomy (140–37 BC), the factionalism of Jewish groups, the entry of Roman might into the east and the force of its imperial hand, Jewish culture in Jesus' day was in the midst of a renaissance and on the cusp of another revolution. Yet, even with these changes there was still a common core to Jewish faith and practice: God, Torah, and temple.

With regard to Jewish life, the Evangelists often assume that their audiences are knowledgeable of it. For this reason, they do not stop to unpack the Jewish world at every turn. When something is unknown, the Evangelists normally provide some explanation: for example, Mark translates for his readers the two occasions where he uses Aramaic terms, signaling that his readers do not know the language (5:41; 7:34). That notwithstanding, the Gospels' depiction of a Jewish pietist from the Galilee naturally betray their role as a source for 1st-century Jewish life.

Languages of the First Century AD. The Gospels originate in a trilingual environment, Greek, Aramaic, and Hebrew. Despite being written in *koiné* ("common") Greek—the *lingua franca* of the eastern Roman Empire—as one moved to a more eastern context, Aramaic and, perhaps, more importantly, Hebrew continued to be spoken within Jewish communities. While both Aramaic and Greek have been staples in New Testament scholarship, Hebrew still lacks equal attention. Yet, there is now a consensus among philologists that Hebrew was indeed alive and well.[22] It was not simply a holy language limited to religious texts. This trilingual environment is attested in the Dead Sea Scrolls: the majority of the nearly thousand scrolls were written in Hebrew, especially those that were authored by the community at *Khirbet Qumran*. The next largest collection is an important cache of Aramaic documents that primarily emerge from east of the land of Israel. Finally, there are a relatively small number of texts composed in Greek.

Indeed, some of the sources used by the Evangelists originate in a Semitic environment, Aramaic (see "Ephphatha" [εφφαθα] in Mark 7:34) and Hebrew. For example, in the narrative of "John's Preaching of Repentance," the Baptist states "Bear fruit that befits repentance, and do not presume to say to yourselves, 'We have Abraham as our father'; for I tell you, God is able from these stones to raise up sons to Abraham" (Matt 3:8–9; Luke 3:8). The passage contains a wordplay between "sons" and "stones" that makes the best sense in Hebrew, but also works in Aramaic. In Greek there are differing words for both sons and stones (*lithoi/uioi*: λίθοι/ υἱοί), but the wordplay is obvious in Aramaic, *bᵉnin* and *abnin* (בְּנִין/אַבְנִין), and Hebrew, *banim* and *ebanim* (בָּנִים/אֲבָנִים), thereby making sense of the Baptist's emphasis on God's power to raise true followers.

Some texts cannot be otherwise understood in any other language than Hebrew. Scholars have already noted that the Gospels are full of post-biblical Hebraisms[23]—Hebrew syntax or terminology that is present in the Greek of the Gospels—that are not the result of Greek translations, like the Septuagint, or attested in biblical Hebrew. These preserve a style of Hebrew that developed in the Second Temple period. For example, the idiom "flesh and blood," which is intended to describe a human being, is a phrase that appears for the first time in manuscript A (6r:8) of Ben Sira, "Like flourishing leaves on a spreading tree which sheds some and puts forth others, so are the generations of flesh and blood" (*basar ve-dam*: בשר ודם; *sarx kai haima*: σὰρξ καὶ αἷμα; 14:18, 17:31; also *m. Sot.* 8:1). This terminology is not inherently Greek, and appears so in Ben Sira because it is a Greek translation of a Hebrew original. The same phrase appears again in Matt 16:17, "And Jesus answered him, 'Blessed are you, Simon Bar-jona! For flesh and blood (σὰρξ καὶ αἷμα) has not revealed this to you….'"

Another discernible example of this appears in Matthew 6:1: "Beware of practicing your righteous (*dikaiosune*: δικαιοσύνη) before men in order to be seen by them…." Verse 2 defines "righteousness" as alms/charity, "So, when you give alms…" (*eleemosune*: ἐλεημοσύνη). In Greek, however, "righteousness" (*dikaiosune*) does not mean charity as it often expresses one of the four Greek virtues (i.e., temperance, prudence, courage, righteousness). In Hebrew, the matter is quite different; by the late Second Temple period, *tzedaqah* (צדקה; i.e., "righteousness") came to refer specifically to "charity/almsgiving" (see Sir 3:30).[24] In the Mishnah, *tzedaqah* is the term used generally for charity (e.g., *gabbaei tzedaqah*: גַּבָּאֵי צְדָקָה=charity collectors; *m. Dem.* 3:1). This is not the language situation in the early Roman period; there it was still employed to refer to inter-relational "justice" (e.g., 1QS 11:5) as it does in the Hebrew Bible (e.g., Jer 4:2). It suggests that the Hebrew (Semitisms) underlying some of the Gospel texts does not mimic that of the Bible, but is a witness to the evolution of meaning that one finds in Jewish texts outside of the Gospels.

Alexander the Great in Battle of Issus (from mosaic found at Pompeii) (photo Berthold Werner, via Wikimedia Commons).

John the Baptist, mosaic in Hagia Sophia, Istanbul (photo Maureen Farrell García).

Charity box with "righteousness" (= charity) written in Hebrew (photo Maureen Farrell García).

Birth of Christ, 19th-century lithograph by M. Fanoli, after J. Führich (via Wikimedia Commons).

Cornice of 3rd-century basalt stone synagogue at Chorazin (photo Maureen Farrell Garcia)

Olive press in a cave dwelling at Beth Guvrin (photo Bukvoed, via Wikimedia Commons).

First-century cave dwelling in Nazareth (photo Jeffrey P. García).

Church of the Nativity in Bethlehem. The steps on the left show that the traditional site is located within a cave (photo Darko Teper Donatus, via Wikimedia Commons).

The Birth of Jesus and Jewish Home Life. Luke states that as a result of the census of Quirinius, Joseph returned with Mary, who was with child, to his home city of Bethlehem in Judea (2:3). The Evangelist then notes, "and while they were there" (*egeneto de en to einai autous*: Ἐγένετο δὲ ἐν τῷ εἶναι αὐτοὺς) Mary went into labor (v. 4). The statement regarding Jesus' birth, "And she gave birth to her first-born son and wrapped him in swaddling cloths, and laid him in a manger, because there was no place for them in the **inn**," has accrued layers of Christian tradition, in particular, due to the translation of the final word "inn" and reference to a "manger" (*fatne*: φάτνη; i.e., an animal trough). Often what is envisioned is a nativity scene that involves a wooden or stone barn that is isolated from family and friends. Understanding the story naturally requires considering how ancient Jews lived in Bethlehem and in other areas of the land of Israel. Excavations have shown that houses in first-century Jewish villages and towns were often built with local stone; for example, the homes and buildings in Chorazin and Capernaum were primarily constructed of local basalt (black volcanic) stone. Some of these basalt homes are in the *insula* style, where several residences are built around a central courtyard. Often these homes were shared by extended families. In Bethlehem and Nazareth, it is clear that homes were completely, or in part, constructed out of interconnected cave systems. Specifically, for Bethlehem, despite the centuries of ornate decorations in the Church of Nativity, pilgrims visiting the traditional location of Jesus' birth still get a sense that they are walking down into a cave. The same types of homes can be seen, without the church tapestries, under the Church of the Annunciation in Nazareth, as well as in the limestone cave systems at Beth Guvrin/Maresha. These homes were often divided between the hearth or clay oven and livestock on one level—the family's livestock would provide warmth during the cooler rainy season—and the family's bedrooms on the upper levels (in the summer families would sometimes sleep on the roofs of the homes).

Awareness of how Jewish communities lived in antiquity helps one to re-address Jesus' birth story. Again, traditionally, he was born alone, humble, isolated from the rest of Bethlehem—his own people. Jesus, Mary, and Joseph are displaced to a barn because the "inn," where payment may have secured a place to stay, had no vacancies. The problem here is that "inn" is not a proper translation of the Greek word *katalumati* (καταλύματι). Stephen Carlson has already correctly argued that the Greek should be translated, "place to stay."[25] Furthermore, Luke suggests that Joseph needs to return to his ancestral home and is already there when Mary goes into labor. Certainly, Joseph's return to Bethlehem in light of the census implies that he would have his family's home to stay. Thus, it is unlikely that they were in need of another place, or *inn*, especially if Joseph's family received word that he was returning with his betrothed.

Indeed, it would have been normal for Joseph's family to have prepared a marital place for Mary, Joseph, and child—one that was an addition to the home. Middle Eastern customs, up to the modern day, indicate that when a son marries, additions would be made to the house in order to accommodate the growing family. This addition could easily be referred to in Greek as a κατάλυμα (*kataluma*; i.e., "lodging/place to stay," traditionally translated as "inn"). For whatever reason, when the time came for Mary to give birth there was no space in that part of the house. As a result, it was necessary to move to the larger part of the home, the area in the cave where the family's oven would be, but also where the family would have kept some of their livestock. What separated the animals from the rest of this room were mangers. Therefore, rather then being abandoned to an isolated barn, born among animals with no one but Mary and Joseph, Jesus is born with Joseph's family not apart from them. While this is not explicitly stated in Luke, the reader must remember that the Gospels, in general, assume that their respective audiences have some familiarity with life in the first century. Taking into account the cultural and linguistic setting of the time, refreshes the traditional reading of the Nativity story.

Jewish Clothing and the Gospels. On three occasions the Gospels make reference to the fringes of Jesus' garment (*kraspedon*: κράσπεδον; Matt 9:20; Luke 8:44/Matt 14:36; Mark 6:56; [Pharisees] Matt 23:5). This Greek word can simply mean the "hem" or "border" of a garment but is also used in the Greek translation of the Hebrew Bible to translate *tzitzit* (צִיצָה, Num 15:38–39; see also, *kanfot*: כַּנְפוֹת, Deut 22:12), which are the ritual fringes required in the Torah to be worn on the four corners of men's garments. As Jodi Magness has noted, Matthew's description regarding the Pharisees who make their phylacteries broad and fringes long can only be speaking about *tzitzit*. Therefore, the Gospels are not referring to the simple hem of a garment but to these ritual fringes on the four corners of an observant Jewish man's mantle. That "mantle" (*himation*: ἱμάτιον) was a large square cloth with four corners. Jews who wore *tzitzit*, as Jesus is depicted doing, would have had them attached to this garment following biblical legislation. The mantle was worn over a "tunic" (*chiton*: χιτών; *kutonet*: כֻּתֹנֶת; e.g., Gen 37:3).

Samuel and David dressed in contemporary-styled mantles (fresco from the 3rd-century synagogue of Dura Europos).

Little can be said about how far wearing *tzitzit* penetrated into first-century Jewish society. In fact, Zeev Safrai has speculated that putting *tzitzit* on garments was not a typical style of Jewish dress. In that sense, there was nearly nothing that outwardly distinguished Jewish dress from other types. It should be noted that the well known *yarmulke*/*kippah* (skull cap) worn by some Jews was not part of ancient dress but developed in the medieval period. While more evidence is needed, the wearing of *tzitzit* was probably done by those who were particularly cautious regarding the application of Torah commandments to their style of dress.

The Pharisees, Sadducees, and Jesus. The Gospels depict Jesus' engagement with several Jewish groups that we know of from extra-biblical sources. Most of these encounters are the result of questions from Pharisees in response to miraculous acts or perceived breaches of the Jewish law (e.g., Matt 12:1–8; Mark 2:23–27; Luke 6:1–5/Matt 15:1–8; Mark 7:1–9; Luke 11:37–54/Luke 16:14–15). Depending on which Gospel, the Sadducees are sometimes present in those same accounts (cp. Matt 16:1–4; Mark 8:11–13). Sadducees, however—that is, the priestly leadership—do not seem to be frequent opponents in Jesus' Galilean ministry but, in fact, play a much larger role in the Passion narratives as they are responsible for handing Jesus over to the Romans (see Matt 26:3; Mark 15:1; esp. Luke 22:66, 23:4). The Evangelists already assume that the reader knows who these groups are and offer little additional information as to their origins, depicting them as an integral part of Jewish society.

Josephus tells us that there were four philosophies within Judaism. The three main groups were the Pharisees, Sadducees, and Essenes, with the Zealot ideology likely being the fourth philosophy. These groups originate in the Hasmonean period. It is clear, that both the Pharisees and Sadducees play some role in the Hasmonean political spectrum. Josephus speaks of the former supporting the Hasmonean queen, Shelomtzion (Salome) Alexandra (76–67 BC; *War* 1:110), while her husband, Alexander Yannai (Jannaeus), was a supporter of the Sadducees (see "The Hymn of King Jonathan" [4Q448]).[26]

The first-century historian also tells us that the main differences between the three groups were their views of fate and free will: the Sadducees believed that all was left to free will; the Essenes, all was left to fate; the Pharisees attempted to strike a balance (see *Ant.* 18:12–26). The fourth philosophy, which is not a single, or specific, group, developed the idea that Jewish political autonomy should be taken by force from the Romans. The actual size of these Jewish groups may have been relatively small during the time of Jesus, but Gospel accounts and other texts suggest a sustained societal influence in the land of Israel. Moreover, while the rise of rabbinic Judaism is complex and no single line of continuity can be drawn, the Pharisees are viewed, in some regard, as the surviving party from which the rabbis evolve after the destruction of Jerusalem in AD 70. To complicate matters further, it seems that underneath the Pharisaic umbrella there existed a variation of opinion, e.g., priestly, zealot, and Hasidic (see below).

Pharisees. In the Gospels the Pharisees are generally portrayed as a group of Jewish teachers of the Torah who are identified primarily with their role in engaging Jesus with questions about Torah observance. Scholars have suggested that their name develops from the verb *parash* (פרש, "to separate"; so, *perushin*: פְּרוּשִׁין) because they maintain a strict sense of ritual purity during meals. Their name was not a self-designation, but was a name used by their opponents (*m. Yad.* 4:6). The Apostle Paul (Phil 3:5) identifies himself as one, having studied with another Pharisee known from rabbinic sources, Gamaliel (Acts 5:35). This is likely the same Gamaliel remembered as "Rabban Gamaliel" in the Mishnah (*m. Ber.* 1:1). The Pharisees are partly associated with the Sages of Israel (*chachamim*: חכמים). Josephus describes them as being more religious than other sects and more accurate interpreters of the law (*War* 1:110). For all of the negativity associated with the Pharisees in Christian tradition, readers often bypass Jesus' positive statement about them in Matt 23:2–3: "The scribes and the Pharisees sit on Moses' seat; so practice and observe whatever they tell you." The verse is a statement regarding the Pharisees' authority to teach Torah. Despite Jesus' stinging critiques against them, these criticisms are not necessarily about their teachings but their actions. Moreover, Gamaliel, a Pharisee, is depicted as a defender of the Jesus movement (Acts 5:34) and the Pharisees appear as early members of the nascent messianic community (15:5).

Replica of the Seat of Moses with Aramaic inscription, from the synagogue remains at Chorazin (photo Maureen Farrell García).

Indigo dyed piece of wool from the Cave of the Letters which may resemble the kind of color used in tzitziyot *(ritual fringes)* (photo Clara Amit; courtesy of Israel Antiquities Authority).

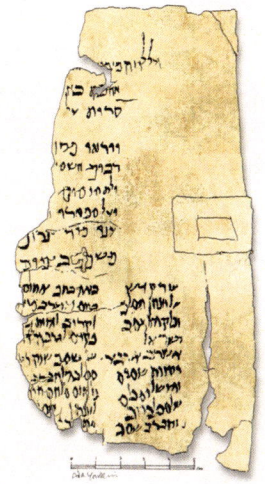

The Prayer for King Jonathan from Qumran. Jonathan is thought by some to be none other than Alexander Yannai (drawing Ada Yardeni).

Column A
1. Praise the Lord, a Psalm [of
2. You loved as a fa[ther(?)
3. you ruled over [
4. vacat [
5. and your foes were afraid (or: will fear) [
6. …the heaven [
7. and to the depths of the sea [
8. and upon those who glorify him [
9. the humble from the hand of adversaries [
10. Zion for his habitation, ch[ooses

Column B
1. holy city
2. for king Jonathan
3. and all the congregation of your people
4. Israel
5. who are in the four
6. winds of heaven
7. peace be (for) all
8. and upon your kingdom
9. your name be blessed

Column C
1. because you love Isr[ael
2. in the day and until evening [
3. to approach, to be [
4. Remember them for blessing [
5. on your name, which is called [
6. kingdom to be blessed [
7.] for the day of war [
8. to King Jonathan [
(transcription and translation by E. Eshel, H. Eshel, and A. Yardeni)

This inscription, found in excavations at Caesarea, may reflect the movement of the priestly courses from Judea to the parts of the Galilee after the Bar Kokhba period (AD 132–135) (Carta collection).

Storage jar discovered in the caves of Qumran (Walters Art Museum).

David Stream at the oasis of Ein Gedi (photo Wink Thompson).

Hasidim ("pious ones"). Historical sources indicate that the *Hasidim* were a group of Jewish miracle workers and a subset of the larger Pharisaic movement. These are, in all probability, not the *Hasidim* mentioned in Maccabees (e.g., 1 Macc 2:42; 2 Macc 14:6). Certain *Tannaim* (earliest generations of rabbi) seem to have connections with this elusive group (e.g., Haninah Ben Dosa; see also, Honi the Circle Drawer; *Ant.* 14:22; *b. Ta'anit* 23a). Sometimes referred to as "Men of Deeds" (*anshei maaseh*), due to their emphasis on the importance of good deeds over Torah study, they are distinguished because of the immediacy by which God responds to their supplications. Close parallels between them and Jesus imply their existence in the 1st century AD. Shmuel Safrai notes at least four parallels between Jesus' ministry and this group of pietists: (1) miracles; (2) father-son relationship with God; (3) poverty as the ideal state; and (4) emphasis of deeds of loving-kindness and charity.[27]

Sadducees. The upper class of priestly elites, from whom the high priest was selected. They were responsible for the temple in Jerusalem, setting the prices of various sacrifices and administering the 24 priestly shifts (*mishmarot*) that served at the temple (1 Chr 24). Members of the group were—along with the elders and leaders of Jerusalem—according to Luke, the only ones involved in Jesus' mock, false trial (Luke 22:15). Annas, a high priest named in the Gospels (Luke 3:2), ascends to his position shortly after Judea becomes a Roman province in AD 6; his five sons served as high priests after him. His son-in-law, Joseph Caiaphas, was high priest, serving in that office for nearly twenty years and played a critical role in handing Jesus over to the Romans.

Qumran Community. Self-identified as the *yaḥad* (i.e., the community) or the "sons of light," this group developed from a priestly schism. The initial break with the priests in Jerusalem was a result of opposing interpretations of the Jewish law. Lawrence Schiffman argues that the Qumran view of the Jewish law most resembles what is ascribed to the Sadducees in rabbinic literature.[28] Once led by the "Teacher of Righteousness," the group believed that they had received the true interpretation of the commandments which were revealed by God to the teacher and hidden from everyone else. The texts discovered in the caves near Khirbet Qumran attest to a group that was deeply concerned with ritual purity, supplemented by messianic and apocalyptic hopes that God would respond to their observance and separation by revealing them to be the true Israel and destroying their enemies. The *yaḥad* of Qumran have a good deal in common with the Essenes, but there are differences as well.

Essenes. A group often associated with the *yaḥad* of Qumran, although this name only appears in Classical sources (e.g., Josephus, Pliny the Elder). They are described by Josephus as believing in immortality of the soul, made use of several sorts of ritual purifications, and spent time reading the holy books and discussing the prophets. Josephus describes another group of Essenes that held these beliefs but disagree on issues of marriage (*War* 2:159–160). Pliny places this group at Ein Gedi, a site that lies south of Khirbet Qumran (*His. Nat.* V).

As mentioned before, the Gospels suggest that the Pharisees and Sadducees are an integral part of Jewish society. Although there is little evidence to what degree their influence penetrated it, the Gospels surely depict the distinct interest of the Pharisees in Jesus' interpretations of Jewish law and the Sadducean plot in handing him over to the Romans. No one group was in control of Judaism, although the Sadducean monopoly over the Temple Mount and its machinations were as close as one group could get to having religious control, while the Pharisees may have had greater sway in how the people were expected to actually practice these various observances.

The presence of the *Hasidim* in Second Temple society is implied strongly in Jesus' teachings (e.g., Matt 6:1–23, see above). The Qumran group, and the Essenes—if they are, or originate as the same group—are referred in Luke and John with the statement: "…for the sons of this world are more shrewd in dealing with their own generation than the sons of light" (Luke 16:8), and "While you have the light, believe in the light, that you may become sons of light" (John 12:36). The "sons of light" was a common name for the group that resided at Qumran (see *Community Rule* 2:16; 3:13, 24; *War Scroll* 1:1). They also may be referenced in Jesus' critique in Matt 5:43–44, "You have heard that it was said, 'You shall love your neighbor and hate your enemy.' But I say to you, 'Love your enemies and pray for those who persecute you.'" The response may directly address a central point of Qumran ideology: "He is to teach them both to love all the Children of Light (Matt: 'neighbor')—each commensurate with his rightful place in the council of God—and to hate all the Children of Darkness (Matt: 'enemy'), each commensurate with his guilt and the vengeance due him from God" (*Community Rule* [1QS] 1:9–11).

The Baptism and Ritual Immersion

John the Baptist's events (Matt 3; Mark 1; Luke 3:1–21; John 1:19–34) calling upon the Jewish people to repent of their sins and immerse, as an indication of that repentance, reflect, in part, concerns for ritual purity and significance of ritual immersion in the Second Temple period. None of the Evangelists insist on explaining to the audience the ins and outs of ritual purity but assume that their audience(s) are already familiar with this aspect of Jewish life.

In the 1st century AD there was a system of practices which originated and evolved from the laws for ritual purity in the Hebrew Bible. They were based on the idea that the Israelites, and later, the Jewish people, could contract certain impurities from various parts of life (e.g., contact with a corpse or carcasses of living creatures [Num 19:11–12; Lev 11:23–44], bodily discharges, including seminal emission [Lev 15], menstrual flow and childbirth [Lev 12], skin diseases [Lev 13–14], and contact with sacred objects or space [Num 19:1–10; Lev 16:4, 23–24]), thereby preventing them from participating in particular rituals and functioning in the sacred spaces, like the Temple (CD 11:21–22). Certain types of vessels, utensils, and liquids were also susceptible to ritual impurities. In fact, the Dead Sea Halakhic Letter[a] (4QMMT [4Q394] 8 iv 5), makes reference to laws dealing the streams of liquids (5–7; also CD 10:10–13). The laws of purification were intended to rectify these impurities. The process of purification was sometimes related to the degree of impurity contracted. For example, a priest who came in direct contact with a corpse required, among other things, the ashes of a red heifer (Num 19:1–10). In other cases, a period of time had to be observed (Num 19:11) before purification could take place (e.g., a woman's impurity after childbirth).

Generally, all forms of impurity require, at some point, water immersion, fully body, hands, and feet. These types of immersion take place in, or with, living water (*mayim chayim*: מַיִם חַיִּים; e.g., Lev 15:13), that is, fresh flowing water—from a spring or in a lake—and collected rainwater that has not been drawn by human hands. This indicates that the lake of Galilee and the Jordan river, except perhaps where the Jordan mixes with waters from the Yarmuk valley (*m. Par.* 8:10), could be used for ritual immersion. Accordingly, Matthew, Mark, and Luke depict the Baptist by the Jordan—in an area north of the lake—where ritual immersion was appropriate according to Jewish law. As a result of the concern for ritual purity, collecting pools of living water called *miqva'ot* (sing., מִקְוֶה; e.g., Exod 17:19; see *m. Miqw.*) developed in the late Hellenistic and early Roman periods.[29] Many of these have already been excavated at the southern steps of the Temple Mount. These were created specifically to deal partly with the purity needs of the priests, as well the pilgrims that would make their way into the Temple from the south during the three pilgrimage feast days. The discovery of the numerous ritual immersion pools (*miqva'ot*) in homes, towns, and villages throughout the land of Israel, and along pilgrimage routes, suggest that ritual purity was a part of Jewish daily life.

Remnants of a 2000-year-old chalkstone vessel factory in lower Galilee discovered by Yonatan Adler (photo Samuel Magal, courtesy of Israel Antiquities Authority).

Steps leading down to a ritual bath at Qumran (photo Samuel Magal).

Other evidence from the period communicates the importance of ritual purity. First, there is a blossoming limestone (esp., chalkstone) industry due to the fact that it was not susceptible to ritual impurity. Second, Eli Shukron, Ronny Reich, and their team are responsible for the discovery of a clay seal that reads "pure to God," which was likely intended to indicate objects or products that were ritually purified. Third, purity concerns undoubtedly penetrated various groups in the Second Temple period. In fact, John makes reference to stone water vessels (*lithinai hudriai*: λίθιναι ὑδρίαι) in the wedding at Cana, which are explicitly said to be vessels for Jewish rites of purification (*ton katarimou ton ioudaion keimenai*: τὸν καθαρισμὸν τῶν Ἰουδαίων κείμεναι, 2:6).

Ritual impurity, generally, has nothing to do with the sin. The *yaḥad* of Qumran innovatively associated ritual immersion with the inward purification of the Holy Spirit, but ritual immersion completed the process; it did not begin it. After confession and repentance, the spirit would purify the individual and then ritual immersion would take place (1QS 3:1–9). The Baptist, who it has long been debated once belonged to the Qumran community—evidence for which is merely circumstantial—seems to share the idea that ritual immersion was only purifying to the person who had previously confessed and repented. While parallels exist, one should be careful placing John among the *yaḥad*. These ideas may have been more prevalent in Jewish society and not an indication of mutual identification between John and Qumran.

Indeed, the Qumran community was invested in maintaining a stringent regimen of ritual purity. Not only were numerous ritual immersion baths discovered but during Roland de Vaux's excavations, his team also discovered hundreds of plates and bowls. If the Essenes—as described in Classical sources—are the same as the community that resided at Qumran, then the plates and bowls parallel Josephus' description of the Essene community, who apparently ate with separate ware in order to maintain every individual's purity (*War* 2:129–131).

Clay seal with the inscription "Pure to God," discovered near the Western Wall (photo Vladimir Naykhin, courtesy Israel Antiquities Authority).

Second Temple period mikveh from Magdala (photo Jeffrey P. García).

Synagogue inscription from Kursi (Gergesa) (photo Jennifer Munro).

Tefillin (phylacteries) from Qumran that would have been worn during prayer by Jesus and others (Israel Antiquities Authority).

Remains of the 1st-century synagogue at Gamla in the Golan (photo Samuel Magal).

The Synagogue at Nazareth and the Sabbath. In Luke 4:16, Jesus enters the synagogue in Nazareth. The Evangelists tells us that it was on the Sabbath and was his "custom" (*eiotha*: εἴωθα). The account brings us into focus with two important features of Jewish life, the Sabbath and the synagogue.

The Sabbath (*sabbaton*: σάββατον; *shabbat*: שַׁבָּת). Sabbath is the day of rest which occurs on the seventh day of the week, from sundown on Friday until sundown on Saturday evening (*yom ha-shabbat*: יוֹם הַשַּׁבָּת, Exod 20:8; also, Lev 24:8; Deut 5:12). There are several occasions in the Hebrew Bible where it is commanded that the seventh day be kept holy. Genesis provides the reasoning that God himself rested from his work of creation and blessed the day (2:3).[30] The first time that the Sabbath is explicitly referred to as a day of rest is Exodus 16:23. The Sabbath maintains its importance to Jewish observance in the Second Temple period. The book of Jubilees suggests that it is the primary thing which distinguishes the people of Israel from the rest of the world. So sacred is this day that the angels are spoken of as observing it in heaven (2:17). The Sabbath is mentioned no less than forty-five times in the Gospels (some in parallel accounts) and is the reason for many of Jesus' encounters with the Pharisees (see "Healing of the Paralytic": Matt 9:1–8, Mark 2:1–12, Luke 5:17–26; Plucking the Grain of the Sabbath: Matt 12:1–8, Mark 2:23–27, Luke 6:1–5).

The Synagogue. A gathering place for the public reading of Torah and the study of the commandments that developed at some point in the Hellenistic period, both in the land of Israel and in the Diaspora.[31] Several first-century synagogues have already been discovered (e.g., Gamla, Masada, Qiryat Sefer), with the most recent discoveries at Magdala, and at Tel Rekhesh in the lower Galilee by Mordechai Aviam. Synagogues were already in place and part of Jewish society before the First Jewish Revolt (AD 66–70). In fact, there is little evidence that the destruction of the Temple (AD 70) had any effect on the leadership or direction of the synagogue. It was commonly a place for the public reading of scripture. It was not a place for prayer, since communal prayer was often associated with the temple. Therefore, Luke's depiction of Jesus reading from Isaiah in chapter 4 is precisely how the first-century synagogue was utilized. Additionally, it appears that Jewish diaspora communities' distance from the temple had an effect on synagogal practice. This is perhaps the reason why synagogues outside of the land of Israel are sometimes referred to as a "place of prayer" (*proseuche*: προσευχή; Acts 16:13).[32]

Prayer. The Gospels' representation of prayer reflects the spheres of prayer that are also attested in extra-biblical texts, namely, public meetings, in privacy, and at the temple (Matt 6:5–6/Matt 6:7–15; Mark 11:25; Luke 11:1–4/Luke 2:37). Prayer at the temple was offered twice daily along with the daily sacrifices in the morning and late afternoon. Additional prayers were probably offered during the Sabbaths and feast days. Jeremy Penner has suggested that while set prayers were being established, the cultic sacrifice set a temporal guideline although what was said in prayer was under the control of the one praying.[33] Apart from the temple, prayer was generally a private affair,

> And when you pray, you must not be like the hypocrites; for they love to stand and pray in the synagogues and at the street corners, that they may be seen by men. Truly, I say to you, they have received their reward. But when you pray, go into your room and shut the door and pray to your Father who is in secret; and your Father who sees in secret will reward you.
>
> (Matt 6:5–6)

Prayers that were set in the Second Temple period include a morning and evening recitation of the *Sh'ma* (Deut 6:4–9; see Aris. 158–160; *Ant.* 4:212; *m. Ber.* 1:1–2). According to the Mishnah, even the morning recitations were structured around functions of the Temple. These morning and evening prayers were accompanied with phylacteries/*tefillin* (Exod 13:9, 16; Deut 6:8; 11:18; Matt 23:5; *tefillin* texts: 1Q13; 4Q128–48; 5Q8; 8Q3), leather pouches with straps containing scriptural texts—likely from Exodus and Deuteronomy—which fulfilled the commandment in the *Sh'ma*, "And you shall bind them as a sign upon your hand, and they shall be as frontlets between your eyes" (Deut 6:8). Private prayers likely consisted of a sanctification of God's name, thanksgiving, and some sort of supplication. These and other elements that we find in the Lord's prayer (Matt 6:7–15; Luke 11:1–4) are also found in what eventually becomes the *Amidah* (18 benedictions/ *shemonah esrei*).[34] Evidence for public or communal prayers at fixed times also come to us from the Qumran community (1QS 9:26–10:1; 1QHodayot[a] 20:4–11; 4QDaily Prayers).

Women in Jesus' Ministry. It has often been thought that Jesus' direct encounter with women (Luke 10:38–42; John 11:5–16; Luke 8:1–3/Matt 9:18–26; Mark 5:21–34; Luke 8:40–48), or the role that women played in his ministry (Mark 15:40; Luke

23:49/Matt 28:1–8; Mark 16:1–8; Luke 24:1–11; John 20:1–2) was part of the Jesus' counter-Jewish movement. It is readily, and incorrectly, assumed that Jewish life in the first century was inherently misogynistic and that there was a complete separation of the sexes in both the public and religious sphere. However, the Gospels' depiction of women's roles are not representative of a counter-Jewish movement, but rather reflect a core component, and regular part of Jewish life in the first century. The suggestion here is not that men and women lived in an egalitarian utopia, or that negative opinion towards women was lacking (cf. Sir 19:2; also *Wiles of the Wicked Woman* [4Q184])—ancient culture was patriarchal—but transposing the Greco-Roman view of women over to ancient Judaism is misguided. Already in the Hasmonean period, the Jewish people were ruled by a queen, Shelomtzion (Salome) Alexandra, who ruled for almost ten years (76–67 BC). The post-biblical book of Judith depicts a Jewess heroine who defeated the Babylonian envoy, Holofernes, by decapitating him. Additionally, we know from a collection of 2nd century AD texts of a woman by the name of Babatha who inherited a date farm from her father and continued to be its primary administrator. Among the documents from this archive are court petitions against the guardians of her orphan son, Jesus, which indicates that there were women, although small in number, who owned land and had certain rights in the larger judicial system.

While it seems that opinions regarding women differed among Jewish communities, and women did not function in the priesthood or have a Levitical role, according to Tal Ilan married women could testify (*Community Rule*[a] 1:10–11), hold leading roles in synagogues, are referred to as "elders" (1Tim 5:1–2),[35] and could become full-fledged members of particular sects.[36] Additionally, while women may have found a common role in the home, there is no archaeological or literary evidence from the Second Temple period that women were separate from men. Luke offers additional portrayals of women as participants and financial supporters of Jesus' ministry (Luke 8:1–3). The accounts of Mary and Elizabeth suggest that both were familiar with the text of scripture. First, when Mary is told that she is with child she utters a canticle called the "Magnificat" (Luke 1:46–55), which closely parallels Hannah's song in 1 Samuel 2:1–10. There Hannah, like many, rejoices for an unexpected child and the opening of her womb. Whether Mary's song is historical or not, it indicates a willingness of the Evangelist to place a song on the lips of a woman which betrays a knowledge of biblical texts. In Luke, Elizabeth says, "Thus the Lord has done to me in the days when he looked on me, *to take away my reproach* (*afelein oneidos mou*: ἀφελεῖν ὄνειδός μου) among men" (Luke 1:25), which bears some linguistic similarity to the miraculous opening of Rachel's womb in Genesis 30:23, "God has taken away my reproach" (ἀφελεῖν ὁ θεός μου τὸ ὄνειδος / אָסַף אֱלֹהִים אֶת־חֶרְפָּתִי). There is little reason to read these as the creation of the author, since they are not exact quotations and it would

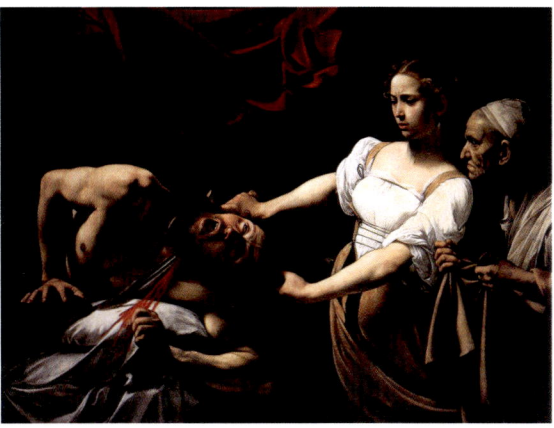

Judith Beheading Holofernes *by Caravaggio, c. 1602.*

be reasonable to presume that both Jewish women knew the stories of Hannah and Rachel. Indeed, both indicate that Mary and Elizabeth have some understanding of the Hebrew Bible. While the lack of historical sources stops one from saying anything about their education, they may have participated in the communal study of biblical texts.

A Pre–70 Passover Meal, but not a *Seder*. Matthew, Mark, and Luke portray Jesus having a Passover meal, that is, a meal which involved the blessing of wine (*cos rishon*: כוס ראשון; *m. Pesah.* 10:2), bread, a meal that included the *pesach* (Passover) lamb, and the recitation of the Hallel psalms (Psalms 113–118). The name of the sacrifice, *pesach* (פסח; e.g., *m. Pesah.* 3:7), was also that of the holiday (*Ant.* 9:271). When Jesus states, "I have earnestly desired to eat this Passover with you…" (*epithumia epethumesa touto to pascha fagein meth humon*: ἐπιθυμίᾳ ἐπεθύμησα τοῦτο τὸ πάσχα φαγεῖν μεθ᾽ ὑμῶν…), he is referring to the roasted lamb that now sits on the table. During Jesus' time, the sanctity of the temple extended to the entire walled city of Jerusalem. Jesus' preparation for the Passover meal within the walls of the city fits these legal requirements (Matt 26:17; Mark 14:13; Luke 22:10). John's description, "before the Passover," indicates that the lamb has yet to be roasted on the temple's altar and cannot, therefore, be a Passover meal which occurred on

A papyrus document from the Babatha Archive discovered in the Cave of the Letters (via Wikimedia Commons).

Samaritan priests celebrating the Passover sacrifice on Mount Gerizim (photo Flavo, via Wikimedia Commons).

The Last Supper by Simon Ushakov, 1685.

15th-century Haggadah by Israel b. Meir of Heidelberg.

Tyrian half-shekel. (left, obv.) Head of Heracles, AD 15–16; (right, rev.) eagle standing on the prow of a ship. Greek inscription reads "Of Tyre, holy and city and asylum" (photo Hanay, via Wikimedia Commons).

the evening (a new day) after the head of the family offered the lamb that was to be eaten (14th Nisan [sacrifice]/15th Nisan [meal])—this practice occurs on the same days every year.

Some scholars argue that John best represents the historical reality. Others suggest that John's calendar reflects the *yaḥad* of Qumran, who based their Passover meal on a solar, rather than a lunar, calendar. The weight of evidence, however, indicates that Matthew, Mark, and Luke have rightly communicated the historical reality. That Jesus and his family were yearly pilgrims during the Passover feast day, and that Jesus is portrayed often as a pilgrim, suggests strongly that he would have participated in accordance with the temple calendar (14th/15th of Nisan). Luke's additional detail tells us that they all "reclined" (*anapipto*: ἀναπίπτω) to eat the Passover meal; Jesus blessed the wine, then the bread (Luke 22:14–23), and all are depicted as sharing from a common dish (Matt 26:23). All of these aspects are contrary to the manner in which the Qumran community (and even the Essenes) celebrated the feast day: (1) they blessed the bread before the wine; and (2) they did not share dishes, each member was given his own ware.

The one distinction that needs to be made with Jesus' Passover meal is that it was not a *Seder* (Heb. "order")—the name commonly used for the Passover meal—and only resembles the modern-day *Seder* in that wine and bread maintain a presence in the ritual (although there are more cups now). The developments that led to the modern-day *Seder*, especially that of the *haggadah*, began in the early rabbinic period.[37]

Jerusalem's Temple. The account of the "Cleansing of the Temple" appears in all four Gospels (Matt 21:12–17; Mark 11:15–19; Luke 19:45–48; John 2:13–16). This is perhaps the most compelling account between Jesus and the leaders of the Jewish religious establishment. It answers several important questions about Jesus: (1) how did he interpret the Scriptures; (2) what was the central thrust of his critique; and (3) towards whom was his most stinging critique directed? In general, Luke provides the fullest, most well-balanced portrayal of the temple. In his Gospel, the Evangelist records Mary's and Joseph's appearance at the temple after Jesus' birth (Luke 2:27). It is also the place to where Jesus and his family would make yearly pilgrimages (2:41). In particular, towards the end of his ministry, Jesus spends his days teaching within the confines of the temple (19:47; see also 7:14). In Matthew, Mark, and John, the temple is painted in an increasingly more negative hue. In Matthew, the first time one reads of the temple, Jesus is being tempted by the devil (4:5). The "Cleansing of the Temple" account is the first time the temple is mentioned in Mark (11:11). And in John's Gospel, the cleansing occurs very early in Jesus' ministry (2:12).

Temple. The temple was the religious center for Jews around the world. Jewish men were required to pay a yearly tax (a half-shekel) for temple upkeep and maintenance (Matt 17:24; *Ant.* 18:313;

Aerial view of the present-day Temple Mount, looking west (photo Andrew Shiva).

also, Exod 30:15; Neh 10:33–34). It was also the location of three annual pilgrimages, *Pesach* (Passover), *Shavuot* (Feast of Weeks, also Pentecost), and *Sukkot* (Feast of Tabernacles). Both Jesus and Paul are depicted observing some of these feasts (Luke 22:1; Acts 20:16; 1Cor 16:8).

The temple of the 1st century AD was renovated and expanded by Herod the Great (beginning in 19 BC). These architectural upgrades were completed long after Herod's death and shortly before the Temple's destruction in AD 70. Many of these expansions can still be seen today. These enhancements consist, among other things, of the expansion of the temple platform to a size of nearly 145 acres (about 24 football fields). The platform on the southern end was suspended over the southern slope of Jerusalem's eastern hill. Within the open space under the flat platform there were massive amounts of fill and in some places a series of vaults that allowed for several subterranean passages. The temple proper was overlaid with gold and marble. So beautiful was the temple that that rabbis would say, "Whoever has not seen Herod's building has not seen a beautiful building in his life" (*b. B. Bat.* 4a). The platform is now occupied by al-Aqsa mosque (Islam's third holiest site) and the Dome of the Rock (a shrine built in honor of Mohammed's journey to heaven). One of Herod's greatest feats was the Royal Stoa, constructed along the southern wall of the mount. It was a massive portico that Josephus describes in detail:

> Now the columns (of the portico) stood in four rows, one opposite the other all along—the fourth row was attached to a wall built of stone,—and the thickness of each column was such that it would take three men with outstretched arms touching one another to envelop it; its height was twenty-seven feet, and there was a double molding running round its base. The number of all the columns was a hundred and sixty-two, and their capitals were ornamented in the Corinthian style of carving, which caused amazement by the magnificence of its whole effect. Since there were four rows, they made three aisles among them, under the porticoes. Of these the two side ones corresponded and were made in the same way, each being thirty feet in width, a stade in length, and over fifty feet in height. But the middle aisle was one and a half times as wide and twice as high, and thus it greatly towered over those on either side. The ceilings (of the porticoes) were ornamented with deeply cut wood-carvings representing all sorts of different figures. The ceiling of the middle aisle was raised to a greater height, and the front wall was cut at either end into architraves with columns built into it, and all of it was polished, so that these structures seemed incredible to those who had not seen them, and were beheld with amazement by those who set eyes on them.
>
> (*Ant.* 15:413–417)[38]

The lower courses of the western wall belong to Herod the Great's plans but some parts of the retaining walls were completed after Herod's death. Remnants of one of the largest free-standing arches in the ancient world, discovered by Edward Robinson, can now be seen from a first-century street that dates to just after the time of Jesus. Eli Shukron discovered that this street, fully uncovered in the 1990s, was a later addition above the original street. The system of *miqva'ot* at the, partly restored, southern monumental staircase are still visible and follow the route where pilgrims would have entered the Temple Mount. This is also likely the setting of Luke's story

(top) Scale model of the Herodian temple, looking east, now on display at The Israel Museum, Jerusalem. The Royal Stoa is the red-roofed building in the model that sits south of the temple (photo Jeffrey P. García).

(above) The Dome of the Rock (photo Maureen Farrell García).

Robinson's Arch (photo Jeffrey P. García).

(top) First-century street along the western wall of the Temple Mount (photo Jeffrey P. García).

(above) The southern steps of the Temple Mount (photo Oren Rozen, via WIkimedia Commons).

Reconstruction of opus sectile flooring from Herod's Jerusalem Temple and perhaps similar to the type of flooring in his Jerusalem palaces. This may be what John describes as the lithostrotos (courtesy Temple Mount Sifting Project).

where Jesus is sitting among the sages when he was twelve (Luke 2:41–52).

Entry to Herod's expanded platform, and the temple proper, occurred through subterranean passages, which are now controlled by the *Waqf* authority—the Jordanian trust that has jurisdiction over the Temple Mount. More recently, the Temple Mount Sifting Project, directed by archaeologist Gabriel Barkay, discovered opus sectile tile work—stones, sometimes precious and polished, that were cut into geometrical shapes—which were inlaid into walls and floors and would have adorned the floor in both the open court of Herod's temple (*War* 5:178) and his Jericho palace. Notley has recently suggested that John's use of the term *lithostrotos* (λιθόστρωτος), when describing where Jesus stood before Pilate (John 19:13), refers to these stones, common in Herodian palaces and likely laid in Herod the Great's *praetorium* (Matt 27:27; Mark 15:16; John 18:28; also Acts 23:25) in Jerusalem.

Priesthood. The priests were a class of men who were responsible for numerous functions, both civic and religious, in the temple. The priesthood, specifically the high priest, reached its pinnacle of power during Hasmonean rule (140–37 BC), in particular the lengthy reign of Alexander Jannaeus (103–76 BC)[39] who named himself both the high priest and king. Under Herod the Great and the Romans, the priesthood lost a good deal of its power, but the party of the Sadducees remained at the upper echelon of society[40] and maintained a heavy hand of control over the temple's internal functions. This authority was solidified by the high priest (Annas) and his family working closely with Rome. In particular, the high priest Caiaphas—Annas' son-in-law—and the Roman prefect Pontius Pilate who were likely in league with one another.

The priestly Sadducean leadership of the Second Temple period is especially known for their corruption, amassing wealth from the inflation of prices for sacrifices and their oligarchy over the temple. The divisions of priests who worked at the temple suffered as a result of this corruption. Josephus tells us that lower-level priests were starving because they were not receiving the grain from tithes which was rightfully theirs (*Ant.* 20:206–207). Both Jesus and the sages of Israel were openly critical of the high priest and other chief priests (see Luke 19:45–48; 20:9–19; *m Ker.* 1:7).

The high priest was responsible for going into the Holy of Holies once a year on the Day of Atonement. The priesthood—that is, the lower priests—were divided into 24 divisions (*mishmarot*; see 1 Chr 24–26; *t. Ta'an.* 4:2). While a certain percentage of these priests lived in Jerusalem, the others were scattered throughout Judea. Among other things, they would officiate the sacrifices at the altar. They were separate from Levites (see *Ant.* 11:181), who, according to Lester Grabbe, helped the priests with the sacrifices but did not function at the altar.[41] Luke tells us that John's father, Zechariah, was a priest of the division of Abijah (1:5), referenced both in 1 Chronicles (24:10) and the reconstruction of the *mishmarot* listed in the Caesarea inscription.

Crucifixion and Death. With life comes death. Crucifixion was implemented by Rome as a form of capital punishment that helped to maintain control over the empire. This method was also employed by the Hasmonean king Alexander Yannai (Jannaeus) and advocated by the Dead Sea community as punishment for a traitor (*Temple Scroll* [11QT] 64: 7–11). Jesus' crucifixion, along with two thieves (Matt 27:33–37; Mark 15:22–26; Luke 23:33–38),

(above) Reconstructed room from one of the priestly homes in Jerusalem's Jewish Quarter that is dated to the Herodian period (photo Deror Avi, via Wikimedia Commons).

(right) Frescoes like this from a Roman villa were signs of wealth and opulence. Similar frescoes were found in the priestly homes in Jerusalem (photo Jeffrey P. García).

Caiaphas' ossuary, on display in The Israel Museum (photo Jeffrey P. García).

represents only a small number of the Jewish people who were tortured and killed in this way. Josephus tells us that thousands of Jews were killed by being crucified before and during the first Jewish revolt.[42] So common was crucifixion that the historian tells us of the soldiers who for amusement nailed the rebels in different postures (*War* 5:451). Yet, it seems that affixing people to the cross by "nails" in the land of Israel was a later innovation that occurred just prior to the first revolt. The only archaeological evidence that we have for crucifixion likely comes from this time. In the tombs of northern Jerusalem, at a site called Giv'at haMivtar, a crucified heel bone was discovered in an ossuary inscribed with the name Yehochanan.

Ossuary inscribed with the name Yehochanan and in which a crucified heel bone was found (photo Jeffrey P. García).

Indeed, not much is known about methods of crucifixion in the 1st century AD. One can tell from the Greek terminology for crucifixion, *staurow* (σταυρόω) and *anastaurow* (ἀνασταυρόω), as well as the Hebrew *talah* (תלה; "hang"), that some kind of stake (*stauros*: σταυρός) was affixed to the ground and the victim was somehow hung. Moreover, if the Hebrew *talah* is underlying the Greek terms in the Gospel, it indicates that ropes, rather than nails, were the common method of crucifixion before the first Jewish revolt. Just prior to the revolt Josephus shifts his description of crucifixion and begins to utilize the Greek verb "to nail" (*proselow*; προσηλόω; *War* 2:308). The cross beam could be perpendicular to the stake or just below the top of the stake, creating the well known Latin cross. Sometimes a small wooden seat called a *sedicule* would be affixed to the stake in order to prolong the process. There is no specific standard on the posture of the victim and our most descriptive narratives of crucifixion in the ancient world come from the Gospels.[43]

Unfortunately, they too lack explicit detail of the victim's posture. Of course, a standardized method was not the point; it was intended to kill the victim with humiliating savagery, causing, by extension, psychological trauma to all those who witnessed these events. With crucifixion, the embers and fires of revolt were effectively extinguished. Death could come in a number of ways, including asphyxiation or hypovolemic shock.

Burial of the Dead. Death was an ever-present reality in the first century, and numerous Second Temple period tombs have been discovered, including the family tomb of Caiaphas, the high priest involved with handing Jesus over to Pilate, and that of Helene of Adiabene (*m. Yom.* 3:10). Many of the tombs are *kokhim* tombs, large rock-hewn tombs that consisted of an antechamber to prepare the corpse, and several finger-shaped niches (*kokhim*; sing., *kokh*) where the prepared body was laid and left for a year. After that year, the bones of the person were reburied in an ossuary (limestone receptacle for bones of the dead). This style of burial was for those of considerable wealth and was in existence for a short time (2nd cent. BC–1st cent. AD). Other burial methods included simple dirt burials, sarcophagi, and coffins. Joseph of Arimathea's request for Jesus' body, the wrapping of Jesus' body in linen, placing him in a family tomb (Luke 23:50–56; Matt 27:57–61; Mark 15:42–47), and rolling a great stone in front of it (Matt 27:60; Mark 15:46), closely describes the preparation for burial that occurred in Second Temple *kokhim* tombs that have been discovered throughout Jerusalem and its environs. However, because Jesus is placed in the tomb right before the Sabbath (Matt 27:57/Mark 15:42/Luke 23:54), and the women, who return with spices to prepare the body, show up to the empty tomb *after* the Sabbath (Matt 28:1/Mark 16:1/Luke 24:1/John 20:1), Jesus' body is never fully buried in the tomb because he is never placed in one of the niches.

Second Temple period kokhim burial in the Chapel of Joseph of Arimathea in the Church of the Holy Sepulchre, Jerusalem (photo Jeffrey P. García).

Second Temple period kokh tomb on the Mount of Olives (photo Jeffrey P. García).

Although 95 percent of Second Temple period tombs discovered were sealed with a square plug, some, like Herod's family tomb (below) and others, were sealed with circular stones (public domain).

JEWISH STYLES OF TEACHING IN THE GOSPELS

The Gospels preserve first-century styles of teaching that are distinctly Jewish. According to them, Jesus' most prominent styles of teaching break down into three general areas in order of priority: parables, *halakhah*, and biblical interpretation. Parables and halakhic discussions often occurred in public settings (e.g., sermons on the mount and plain), while biblical interpretation occurred in either ("Parable of the Good Samaritan"; Luke 10:25–37).

Parables. The majority of Jesus' teachings come in the form of parables (*parabole*: παραβολή; *mashal*: משל), namely, story parables, which are short narratives that generally involve some sort of comparison. Often the narrative utilizes anonymous characters that present a reality—sometimes an aspect of daily life—which teaches deep, sublime theological matters in a manner that is easily related, palatable, and comprehended. As Brad Young describes, "in finite terms God is beyond human comprehension, but on the other, his infinite majesty may be captured in vivid stories of daily life."[44] Jesus' parables have often been mistaken for secret telling where those outside of his inner circle are told parables in order to keep them from understanding the secrets of his true purpose. But this is not the point of parables in any body of Jewish literature. In fact, parables, as described by Matthew, are used, "…because seeing they do not see, and hearing they do not hear, nor do they understand" (Matt 18:12–13). In other words, parables are intended to give understanding, not mask it.

Jesus' parables are similar to those that are collected in the literature of the *Tannaim*. The earliest traditions account for more than 450 parables. A fully fleshed-out parable will often be made of two components, a *mashal* (i.e., the story parable) and a *nimshal* (i.e., moral message; application). Notley and Zeev Safrai list seven characteristics of a parable: (1) a statement that defines it as a parable; (2) a narrative that is specifically used to teach a moral; (3) it does not include the name of the Sage, his location, where the story took place, etc; (4) the parable describes a certain "reality" where characters appear without names; (5) it generally does not contain divine visions; (6) the moral of the story is spelled out; (7) the parable is told in Hebrew, even in texts that are predominantly Aramaic. Additionally, "A narrative that has all the characteristics is definitely a *mashal*. Any text that has none of them is not a *mashal* [i.e., parable]."[45]

When compared with the Gospels' parables, the aforementioned rabbinic parables provide important methodological nuances for understanding Jesus' favorite teaching methods: (1) rabbinic parables are always written down in Hebrew and are depicted as being taught in Hebrew by the Sages, even a parable that is surrounded by Aramaic commentary; (2) this implies that in Jewish circles, parables were taught in Hebrew, and for the Gospels—even though they are recorded in Greek—they likely originated from Hebrew originals; (3) moreover, the parables of the Sages shed light on possible debates that lie behind Jesus' own parables. For example, the parable in Luke, "The House Built Upon the Rock," contains a comparison that has close parallels to one in rabbinic literature.

The text in *Avot de-Rabbi Nathan* below is interconnected with a number of other parables that seek to answer a question that reverberated throughout the the Second Temple period: which is more important, Torah study or good deeds?

Overlooking the Gennesar plain from Mount Arbel (photo Jeffrey P. García).

"The House Built Upon the Rock" (Matt 7:24-27)	*Avot de-Rabbi Nathan*, ms. A, 23
Every one then who hears these words of mine and does them will be like a wise man who built his house upon the rock; and the rain fell, and the floods came, and the winds blew and beat upon that house, but it did not fall, because it had been founded on the rock. And every one who hears these words of mine and does not do them will be like a foolish man who built his house upon the sand; and the rain fell, and the floods came, and the winds blew and beat against that house, and it fell; and great was the fall of it.	Elisha ben Abuya says, "A man who has good deeds in him and has studied much Torah, to what is he compared? To a man who builds first with stones and afterwards with mud bricks. Even when much water comes and rises up against them, it doesn't dislodge them. A man in whom there are no good deeds, [even though] he has studied much Torah, to what may he be compared? To a man who builds first with mud bricks and afterwards with stones. Even if there is only a little water, immediately they topple over."[46]

Both the Matthean and Lukan versions, though edited by the Evangelists, begin with a similar statement, "Every one who comes to me and hears my words and does them, I will show you what he is like." The Lukan version reads more like the parables that we find elsewhere with the wording, "what he/it is like" (*tini estin homoios*: τίνι ἐστὶν ὅμοιος; Luke 6:47), which is not unlike, "to what is it compared" (*lama hu domeh*: למה הוא דמה). It can be shown that "like" (*homoios*: ὅμοιος) is a proper Greek translation for "compare, like" (*damah*: דמה; Ezek 31:8).

In both Gospels, the statement hinges on one who not only hears but does what Jesus teaches. At first glance, it appears that Jesus is simply speaking of the dangers posed to his followers who do not obey *his* teachings. But there is no specificity to which teachings Jesus refers. Is it simply a catchall for all his teachings? Probably not.

The very close parallel shown above states the matter at hand explicitly: which is more important, good deeds or Torah study? For Elisha ben Abuya, the one who builds—in similar fashion to the Gospels—on rock, or, more specifically, builds first with stone and then with mud bricks, secures his building from the rising waters. This is the one who places good deeds before Torah study. To do the opposite puts the building at risk, for when even a little water arises, the building, founded on mud bricks, is easily destroyed. R. Abuya states that this is the one who has studied Torah but has no good deeds. In a similar fashion, Jesus' parable stresses the importance of "hearing" (study) and "doing" (good deeds). Such a pairing, this time regarding wisdom and deeds, is preserved on the lips of Hanina ben Dosa:

> Rabbi Hanina ben Dosa…would say: Anyone whose deeds are more plentiful than his wisdom, his wisdom endures. And anyone whose wisdom is more plentiful than his deeds, his wisdom does not endure.
>
> (*m. Avot* 3:9)

As a *hasid*, Hanina belonged to those in the Jewish community who emphasized good deeds over "wisdom" (which comes from Torah study). He belongs to a group of wonder working, pious men (i.e., the *Hasidim*) who stressed action on behalf of those in need. Sometimes they were referred to as *anshei maaseh* ("men of deed"). But these deeds were not random action, they were occupied with taking care of the needy and the poor. Of course, Rabbi Abuya and Rabbi Dosa are not against Torah study (or the acquiring of wisdom). The question was one of priority. Action on behalf of those in need supersedes other activities. Indeed, there were those among the rabbis who disagreed (*b. Qidd.* 40b).

The connection between deeds and Torah study/wisdom was intricately tied to interpretations of Exodus 24:7: "All that the LORD has spoken *we will do, and we will hear*" (*naaseh v'nishma*: נַעֲשֶׂה וְנִשְׁמָע).[47] At this point in Exodus, the people of Israel are at Sinai as Moses takes the book of the covenant (*sefer ha-berit*: סֵפֶר הַבְּרִית) and reads it to the people. One would assume that hearing should come before doing, since it is logical that one needs to hear the instructions in order to know what to do. The rather strange reverse order of "we will do, and we will hear" is precisely what attracts interpreters. It is an intentional marker from which meaning on how to live within God's covenant can be attained. In fact, *Avot de-Rabbi Nathan* (ms. A, 18) connects this verse in Exodus with Hanina ben Dosa's statement above regarding wisdom and good deeds: "He used to say, 'Everyone whose deeds exceeds his wisdom, his wisdom is established. Everyone whose wisdom exceeds his deeds, his wisdom is not established.' As it is said, 'We will do and we will hear'" (Exod 24:7). Exodus' mention of "doing" before "hearing" settles the argument that "good deeds" should take priority over Torah story.

Returning to the Gospels, there are indicators that Jesus' parable is tapping into this larger debate and that the Gospels presume that their respective audiences are already aware of it. First, the passages in Matthew and Luke uses two verbs, "hear" (*akouw*: ἀκούω) and "do" (*poeiw*: ποιέω), which nicely parallel Exodus 24's two verbs, "hear" (*shama*: שמע) and "do" (*asah*: עשה). Second, it is clear throughout the Gospels that Jesus puts a heavy emphasis on taking care of those in need (e.g., Matt 6:1, 19:21, 25:31–46; Mark 12:41–44/Luke 21:1–4; Luke 10:29–37, 18:22; see more below). The language of the parable and Jesus' preference for good deeds throughout the Gospels suggests that underlying it is the ancient Jewish debate about which is more important, Torah study or charitable action. Indeed, along with other *Hasidim*, Jesus stressed the importance and redemptive power of charity; good deeds are to be foundational to his followers' piety and their observance of the commandments. In that sense, Jesus, Hanina ben Dosa, and Elisha ben Abuya agree on the priority of good deeds. Moreover, for Jesus, it is taking care of those that are in need which represents the "rock" that is to be built on, the "rock" of doing.

Halakhah[48] (Jewish Law/Commandments).

Some Christian tradition has maintained that Jesus' statement in Matthew, "I have come not to abolish them [i.e., the law and the prophets] but to *fulfill* them" (5:17), indicates that part of his task was to complete the law perfectly—something that no normal human could accomplish—so that the law would no longer be a burden to the followers of the Christ; this is especially thought to relate to the so-called ritual parts of the law (e.g., sacrifices, kosher laws, clothing, purity, etc.). For some New Testament commentators, the so-called ethical portions are still in play (e.g., love God, love neighbor). However, in ancient Judaism, Jewish law is never divided neatly in two separable halves, ethical and ritual—the Torah, its commandments and interpretations comprise a single whole. The book of James bears witness to this understanding, "whoever keeps the *whole law* (=Torah; *holon ton nomon*: ὅλον τὸν νόμον), but fails in one point has become guilty of all of it" (2:10). The commandments in the Torah are an intricate and interconnected body of rituals and ethics; these

Partially reconstructed wall at Tel Beer Sheva with stone foundation and mud bricks (photo Jeffrey P. García).

Jesus with his followers (from William Foster's *The Bible Panorama or The Holy Scriptures in Picture and Story*, 1891).

two categories are the two faces of a single coin, inseparable from one another. To follow one is to follow all; to break one is to break all.

Further, the problem with reading Matthew as an implication that Jewish legal rituals, or the entire law, will come to an end for the followers of Jesus, is that it does not agree with the rest of the passage, especially 6:19–48, and, in particular, "Whoever then relaxes one of the least of these commandments and teaches men so, shall be called least in the kingdom of heaven; but *he who does them* and teaches them shall be called great in the kingdom of heaven" (vv. 19–20). In other words, to teach anyone not to observe the commandments (the entire Torah), however small, poses dangers to those who associate themselves with the kingdom of heaven. Therefore, it is better to translate "fulfill" (Gk. *plerow*: πληρόω) as to give "full meaning."

The rest of the Sermon on the Mount supports this translation, as it teaches about a number of commandments (e.g., adultery, murder, oaths). These verses have often been regarded as anti-law, and referred to as the Antithesis, namely, showing how the Jewish law is usurped by Jesus' authority. However, this anti-law position would not fit comfortably in the world of any first-century Jewish sage. Matt 5: 21–48 depict an interpretation, not an "abolishing" or usurping of Jewish law. For example, Jesus says, "You have heard that it was said, 'You shall not commit adultery.' But I say to you that every one who looks at a woman lustfully has already committed adultery with her in his heart" (vv. 27–28). "It was said" is not unlike what is found in Jewish literature, *neemar* (נאמר, "as it is said," *m. Pe'ah* 6:5), for the quotation of a biblical text. Jesus' addition, "but I say to you," is also similar to the rabbinic, *ani omer* (אני אומר, "I say," *m. Toh.* 3:7), which introduces an interpretation of a particular law. Reading Matthew in this context suggests that Jesus is giving an interpretation of the law, and not doing away with or usurping the authority of Torah.

As with any sage of Israel, Jesus was tasked with the responsibility of distilling and interpreting the Torah's commandments for his followers. In fact, in the above example, he is not challenging the validity of God's commandments, but giving the full meaning, so that his followers would know how to faithfully live in relationship to God and his covenant. The working assumption in the Gospels is that Jesus observes the commandments and expects his followers to do the same. This continues to be the case after the resurrection; that is to say, after Jesus' reported death, resurrection, and ascension, Peter and Paul both continue to follow Jewish law. In Acts 10, Peter tells Jesus, "No, Lord; for I have never eaten anything that is common or unclean" (v. 14). His character is understood as being obedient to kosher food laws. Peter's vision in the Book of Acts of the animals and sheet is not intended to correct the apostle regarding his keeping *kashrut*; it is to show him that God shows no partiality (v. 34) among humanity and that the Gentiles were to be accepted among the early messianic community. Paul, in his observance, ritually immerses and pays for the vows of four Nazirites in Acts 21:23 to show that there was nothing to the controversy that surrounded him, namely, that he was teaching Jews in the Diaspora to not follow the Mosaic law, especially circumcision, the very mark of God's covenant (v. 21). This act of immersion and righteous act of piety toward the four Nazirites was intended to show that Paul continued to live in "observance of the law" (v. 24).

The Gospels' literary identity as "Jewish" is attested with the preservation of a number of halakhic (matters of Jewish law) discussions that occur between Jesus and the Pharisees. Scholars have debated them for years. The most popular among them are the so-called *Sabbath controversies*: accounts where questions arise regarding Jesus' perceived transgression of the commandment to rest and keep the Sabbath holy. The day of rest is an important observance in Judaism (see above). Evidence in the Gospels, and other Second Temple sources, indicate that debates regarding what was allowable on the Sabbath day remained an important part of Jewish life. Thus, the Sabbath controversies are not Jesus' attempt to claim authority over the holy day, but rather, they arise from his interpretations regarding the Sabbath that differ from popular Pharisaic opinion at the time. As one finds in the famous discussions between the Houses of Shammai and Hillel, the slightest difference in the interpretation of a particular commandment can cause debate (e.g., *m. Ber.* 1:3).

The Plucking of Grains on the Sabbath. One of the more prominent halakhic disputes occurs in the account of the "Plucking of Grains on the Sabbath" (Matt 12:1–8/Mark 2:23–28/Luke 6:1–5). This is the only Sabbath controversy that deals with something other than healing. While the Markan account has been treated as the most ancient of the three, elements of the Lukan account, including its terseness—it is the shortest of the three—suggest that the Evangelist has a slightly earlier, or independent, tradition from those of Matthew and Mark, both of which have considerable additions.[49] Luke's reference to the "rubbing" (*psochontes*: ψώχοντες; Luke 6:1) of grains, rather than just "plucking" and "eating"—as it is in all three Synoptic Gospels—is one significant difference.[50] The importance of this halahkic discussion at the time is affirmed by the the laws regarding the rubbing and eating grain that one finds in the Dead Sea Scrolls (*4QHalakha*[a] 9:1; *4QBlessing*[a] 5:1) and early literature of the rabbis (*m. Menah.* 6:5).

The Gospels' accounts are inviting the reader into a contemporary debate regarding plucking/eating grain on the Sabbath. These same discussions occur throughout ancient Jewish literature (e.g., *Jubilees* 50; Philo, *Mos.* 2:2; CD 10:14–11:18;[51] *m. Shabb.* 7:2). The deliberations are a natural part of the Jewish community's desire to properly observe Torah's Sabbath laws. In other words, every Jewish community needs to continually readdress how to keep the Sabbath "holy" by defining what is considered "work," especially amidst societal and communal innovations. The Gospels are a window into these conversations. Jesus offers his own interpretation—a standard method for any sage of the first century—of what is allowed on the Sabbath. Even more, Jesus provides biblical support for his interpretation referring back to 1 Samuel 21:1–6 when David was hungry and partook of the shewbread. It is not uncommon to find other rabbis utilizing David to support their own legal positions (e.g., *m. Sanh.* 2:2).[52]

The Lukan account ends abruptly, "The Son of Man is Lord of the Sabbath" (6:5). Without further explanation, it appears that the Evangelist either did not understand this phrase, or expected his audience to know its meaning. The Markan version adds an important explanatory comment, "The sabbath was made for man, not man for the sabbath," which is very close to the later Talmudic statement, "it [i.e., the Sabbath] is committed to your hands, not you to its hands" (*b. Yoma* 85b). While the Talmudic statement is written down much later than the Markan account, the meaning is the same. There is a certain amount of authority given to humankind in order to determine what matters are prohibited and which are permissible on the Sabbath. The Lukan statement fits under this understanding, as well, if one reads the appearance of the "Son of Man" in its Hebraic sense, *ben adam* (בן אדם), which, among other things, can mean the "every person"—a general reference to the human being. In other words, according to Luke, as we have seen, the authority to shape allowances and prohibitions on the Sabbath is not a question of Jesus' authority but one that is within the authority of "*every* person"/community. The same understanding of *ben adam* appears clearly in Matthew's version of the "Healing of the Paralytic."

> *But that you may know that the Son of man has authority on earth to forgive sins—he then said to the paralytic—"Rise, take up your bed and go home." And he rose and went home. When the crowds saw it, they were afraid, and they glorified God, who had given such authority to men.*
>
> (Matt 9:5–7)

The Matthean version of the "Plucking of Grains on the Sabbath" has an even more pointed reference to what is allowable on the Sabbath, "I tell you, something greater than the temple is here. And if you had known what this means, 'I desire mercy, and not sacrifice,' you would not have condemned the guiltless. For the Son of man is lord of the Sabbath" (Matt 12:6–8). Some have suggested that Jesus here refers to himself as "something greater" (*meizon*: μεῖζόν). But this is grammatically impossible. In Greek, as in many ancient languages, nouns have gender and number; Jesus (*ihsous*; Ἰησοῦς) is masculine, singular, while "something greater" is neuter, singular. Matthew cannot be referring to Jesus because the two terms do not agree in gender as Koiné Greek requires. There is another word, however, in the passage above that is both neuter and singular, "mercy" (*eleos*; ἔλεος). The quotation of Hosea 6:6 is critical to the text; it argues that merciful action takes priority even over the temple. For Jesus, in Matthew and Luke, mercy and deeds of charity are a halakhic, that is, a legal precedent. So too the commandments to love (Deut 6:5; Lev 19:18; 19:34), and the care for interpersonal relationships, take priority over all other commandments. This idea is echoed by the rabbinic statement, "charity and deeds of loving-kindness outweigh all the commandments in the Torah." In other words, it is the disciples' hunger and the opportunity to be merciful to them by satisfying it, that take precedence over Sabbath restrictions.

Jewish Styles of Biblical Interpretation.

Ancient Jewish biblical exegesis is often based on uniqueness of Hebrew language in the Bible. Some of these styles of exegesis were known as *middot* and were attributed to Hillel, a sage that lived about one hundred years before Jesus. The seven *middot* of Hillel appear for the first time, unattributed to any sage, in the Tosefta (*Sanh.* 7:11).

	The seven *middot* of Hillel	שבע מידות דרש הלל לפני זקני בתירה
1	*qal v'homer* (light and heavy; *a minori ad maius*)	קל וחומר
2	*gezerah shavah* (comparison of decrees)	גזרה שוה
3	*binyan av mikatuv echad* (building a principle from a single text)	בנין אב מכתוב אחד
4	*binyan av mishene ketuvim* (building a principle from two texts)	בנין אב משני כתובים
5	*kelal uferat, uferat ukelal* (the general and the particular, the particular and the general)	כלל ופרט, ופרט וכלל
6	*keyotze bo mimaqom akher* (analogy made from another passage)	כיוצא בו ממקום אחר
7	*davar halamed me'inyano* (explanation obtained from context)	דבר הלמד מעניינו

Despite the existence of a Greek translation of the Bible in the first century, and, eventually, several Aramaic versions after the destruction of the temple (AD 70), there is no evidence of ancient Jewish interpreters using any text other than the Hebrew one. Although some of these originated in the Greek world, their full adaptation and inclusion among the sages are irrefutable. Moreover, the actual application of these *middot* does not occur often in Second Temple period texts,[53] and is far more prevalent in rabbinic texts, specifically within halakhic discussions, with a couple of exceptions (4 Ezra 8:42–45; double love commandment, see below).

The Use of Middot *in the Gospels.* Some of the earliest literary witnesses to these *middot* are the Gospels. Already one finds in Matthew the use of *qal v'homer* (light and heavy). In the "Sermon on the Mount," Jesus is recorded as saying in regard to the anxieties of life, "But if God so clothes the grass of the field, which today is alive and tomorrow is thrown into the oven, will he not much more clothe you, O men of little faith?" (Matt 6:30). The care of God for the grass of the field, despite its impermanence, is the light matter. If God's care is true in the light matter, then the more important matter, namely, God clothing the person, is equally so.[54] As part of the Sermon on the Mount, Matt 6:25–34 provides

Healing the Man with the Withered Hand (from 11th-century Hitda Codex).

Wadi Qelt, looking east (photo Jeffrey P. García).

St. George's Monastery sits in Wadi Qelt which leads from Jericho to Jerusalem (public domain).

no explanation for why Jesus' followers might be anxious. It is true that for many in ancient times, life in general was an anxiety-filled enterprise. In fact, there were other rabbis who taught that their disciples should only be concerned with the remains of the day and not with the coming ones. Another way of unraveling the meaning of this passage regarding anxiety is to see it in light of Jesus' teaching of charity. Already in Matt 6:19, one reads about "treasure in heaven" as an ancient idiom for giving charity[55]—and the very chapter begins with, "Beware of practicing your charity before men in order to be seen by them…thus, when you give alms…" (Matt 6:1–2). Therefore, the aforementioned anxiety in Matthew may result directly from the degree of charity that Jesus requires elsewhere. As he says to the rich young man in Matt 19:21, "If you would be perfect, go, sell what you possess and give to the poor, and you will have treasure in heaven." The Lukan version adds the clarifying adjective, "all," indicating how much is required of the rich (see Luke 18:22, also 4:6). The concept of giving "all" would surely cause a great deal of anxiety, since it appears to go beyond the expected 1/5 ratio of assets to charity that the rabbis established. While giving all is not without parallel in ancient Judaism (*b. Ta'an.* 24a), it was not the common ancient Jewish view of charitable giving—such expectations would have naturally caused concern for one's own well-being (e.g., clothing, food, etc.). Jesus' teaching on God's intimate care for his people and our own anxieties about tomorrow makes the most sense when it is connected to the emphasis on charity that appears throughout the sermon and the Gospels.

Another *middah*, *gezerah shavah*—a comparison or analogy of two rulings that share similar words (sometimes exact forms)—occurs in Matthew. When utilized in rabbinic discourse, it is generally part of halakhic discourse, although evidence exists of its use in non-halakhic contexts. The Gospels utilize them generally in matters having to do with Torah observance. The most obvious example is the Double Love commandment—Deut 6:5 and Lev 19:18.

Deut 6:5: *and you shall love (וְאָהַבְתָּ) the LORD your God with all your heart, and with all your soul, and with all your might.*

Lev 19:18: *but you shall love (וְאָהַבְתָּ) your neighbor as yourself: I am the LORD.*

The fusion of these passages is found throughout Second Temple period Jewish sources (*Jub.* 20:2, 7; 36:4–8; *T. Iss.* 5:2; *T. Dan* 5:3; Philo, *Spec. Laws* 2.63; *Sib. Or.* 8:480–82; *Did.* 1:2) and was the result of unique phraseology, "And you shall love" (*ve-ahavta*: וְאָהַבְתָּ). These two passages are Jesus' response to the question, "Teacher, which is the great commandment in the law" (Matt 22:36; Mark 12:28). Of course, by the time of Jesus, Leviticus 19:18's "you shall love your neighbor as yourself," had already attained an esteemed recognition among Jewish communities (Sir 28:2–4; Gal 5:14; James 2:8; cf. Rom 13:9; see also *Avot de-Rabbi Nathan* B 26; *y. Ned.* 9:4; *Gen. Rab.* 9:4). It is especially highlighted in the famous, but later, talmudic story of "Shammai, Hillel, and the Proselyte" (*b. Shabb.* 31a).

The "Parable of the Good Samaritan" (Luke 10:25–37) details a unique innovation regarding the Double Love commandment. In a similar scenario to the "Rich Young Man," Jesus is posed a question regarding what shall be done to inherit eternal life (Luke 10:25). In quintessential Jewish fashion, Jesus asks a question, "What is written in the law? How do you read?" The scholar of Jewish law (*nomikos*: νομικός), replies with the double love commandment, "You shall love the Lord your God with all your heart, and with all your soul, and with all your strength, and with all your mind; and your neighbor as yourself." Yet, in order to correctly understand Jesus' affirmation of the two commandments, the Jewish scholar poses a logical question, "And who is my neighbor?" Jesus then launches into the story of the Good Samaritan:

A man was going down from Jerusalem to Jericho, and he fell among robbers, who stripped him and beat him, and departed, leaving him half dead. Now by chance a priest was going down that road; and when he saw him he passed by on the other side. So likewise a Levite, when he came to the place and saw him, passed by on the other side. But a Samaritan, as he journeyed, came to where he was; and when he saw him, he had compassion, and went to him and bound up his wounds, pouring on oil and wine; then he set him on his own beast and brought him to an inn, and took care of him. And the next day he took out two denarii and gave them to the innkeeper, saying, "Take care of him; and whatever more you spend, I will repay you when I come back." Which of these three, do you think, proved neighbor to the man who fell among the robbers?

(Luke 10:30–36)

Corinthian pillars of the 4th-century limestone synagogue at Capernaum (photo Maureen Farrell García).

Jesus has ingeniously flipped the question on its head by depicting the Samaritan as the hero. The potential of this narrative to be controversial is high, especially considering that the relations between Jews and Samaritans were, at best, tense. Adding insult to injury, a Levite and a priest are depicted as having passed by the injured, nearly dead man.

The story may hinge on the legal designation of what it means to be "half dead," that is, near death but not quite there.[56] One must remember when reading the story that coming in contact with a corpse is the highest degree of impurity, especially for a priest. The depiction of the priest and the Levite may have been a stinging indirect critique against the chief priests who had forgotten their duties to care for the Jewish people, and invested themselves in amassing wealth. Whatever the answer may be, surely the scholar did not expect Jesus to bring a Samaritan into the equation. Yet, it is the Samaritan who does a profound act of mercy to a stranger whose social, ethnic, or national identity are lacking. That this story likely takes place geographically on the well-known road from Jerusalem to Jericho, the very route that Jewish pilgrims would take to avoid traversing through the heart of Samaritan country, is not happenstance. Turnage notes that Samaritans would sometimes harass pilgrims as they made their way to Jerusalem, strongly suggesting that the victim was Jewish.[57]

The more unique departure with this account is that it leads the reader back to the third occasion where *ve-ahavta* appears in the Bible: "The stranger who sojourns with you shall be to you as the native among you, and you shall love him as yourself (*ve-ahavta lo kamocha*: וְאָהַבְתָּ לוֹ כָּמוֹךָ); for you were strangers in the land of Egypt: I am the LORD your God" (Lev 19:34). By the time of the Second Temple, the relative term *kamocha* ("as yourself") comes to be understood, "as one who is like you." In other words, one who shares the same strengths, vulnerabilities, and weaknesses. Certainly, it is beyond coincidence that these passages, which share the same unique language, were brought together; it is not random or coincidental. It purposely upsets expected ethnic and social boundaries, and causes the hearer to come face to face with the dangers of following societal ideologies rather than the commandments to love God, neighbor, and foreigner without exception. In fact, Jesus' response may subtly critique the more restrictive terminology that we find among the *yaḥad* of Qumran, "Each one must love his brother (אחיהו) as himself..." (CD 6:20–21; see also *Jub.* 35:22). The use of "brother" (*ach*: אח) instead of "neighbor" (*re'ah*: רֵעַ) naturally restricts who the Qumran community is expected to love, that is, specifically, those who belong to the "sons of light" (i.e., Qumran community). This idea finds a parallel in another Dead Sea Scroll, the Community Rule, where the "sons of light" are commanded to hate all of the "sons of darkness" (i.e., everyone outside of the community, 1QS 1:9–10). Jesus' interpretation of "neighbor" expands the expectation of merciful actions, and good deeds, beyond communal identity and forcefully challenges these potential limitations by portraying a Samaritan as caretaker of the nearly dead.

The Synagogue at Nazareth and Jewish Biblical Interpretation. While we have several references of Jesus preaching in the synagogues of Galilee (Matt 4:23; Mark 1:39; Luke 4:44), apart from the healings which are associated with lessons, there is only one fully fleshed-out narrative of the biblical content of his preaching (Luke 4:16–30). The parallels to this account in Matthew and Mark do not preserve the teaching, but note that the visitors of the synagogue were astonished (Matt 13:53–58; Mark 6:1–6). Luke reads:

A reconstructed first-century synagogue at Nazareth (photo Ian Scott, via Wikimedia Commons).

Torah scroll not unlike the one Jesus would have unrolled in Nazareth that day (via Wikimedia Commons).

Entrance to the traditional tomb of Honi the Circle Drawer (photo Dr. Avishai Teicher, via Pikiwiki Israel).

And he came to Nazareth, where he had been brought up; and he went to the synagogue, as his custom was, on the Sabbath day. And he stood up to read; and there was given to him the book of the prophet Isaiah. He opened the book and found the place where it was written, "The Spirit of the Lord is upon me, because he has anointed me to preach good news to the poor. He has sent me to proclaim release to the captives and recovering of sight to the blind, to set at liberty those who are oppressed, to proclaim the acceptable year of the Lord." And he closed the book, and gave it back to the attendant, and sat down; and the eyes of all in the synagogue were fixed on him. And he began to say to them, "Today this scripture has been fulfilled in your hearing."

(Luke 4:16–21; RSV)

The Evangelist provides the reader with important details of synagogal practice that Matthew and Mark do not. First, Luke states that going to the synagogue on the Sabbath was a "custom" for Jesus (more on this below). Second, it says, "he stood up to read," which Shmuel Safrai notes is evidence that Jesus also read from the Torah, as well as Isaiah.[58] Standing to read the Torah was required, where reading the prophetic portion, that is the *haftarah*, did not necessarily need to be done while standing.

Jesus opens Isaiah and, at first glance, appears to read only from Isaiah 61:1–2. However, the text in Luke does not follow chapter 61 exactly. There are three differences between the Lukan passage and the prophet: (1) the omission of Isaiah 61:1b, "to bind the brokenhearted"; (2) the omission of Isaiah 61:2b, "And the day of vengeance of our God"; and (3) the insertion of Isaiah 58:6, "and let the oppressed go free." What is interesting for us is the sudden insertion of Isaiah 58:6. It is common for ancient sages to quote terse sections of passages, assuming that the readers were already aware of the complete text. Insertions of a separate text indicates some interpretive ingenuity on the part of the teacher; the speaker moves from quoting and reading to interpreting. The question is, of course, in what manner is this done?

The insertion of Isaiah 58 brings the reader to another interpretive *middah*, as mentioned above, *gezerah shavah*, which interprets one text through another because both share unique wording. Both Isaiah chapters share phraseology that is unique in the Hebrew Bible, *ratzon la-adonai* (רְצוֹן לַיהוָה, will of the Lord). The only two occasions where this appears are in two passages that Jesus brings together.[59] This style of biblical interpretation is not coincidental, as its use reveals the very core of Jesus' message. Isaiah 61 speaks about the "Spirit of the Lord" and touches on the expectation that God would bring an end to the perceived enemies of the community at Nazareth. This is not wholly unlike what the Qumran community expected for the "Sons of Darkness" (see the *Scroll of the War of the Sons of Light Against the Sons of Darkness* [1QM]). But Jesus' quotation in Luke omits the "day of vengeance" (*yom naqam*: יוֹם נָקָם) from Isaiah 61:2. In fact, he is challenging this ideology by inserting a portion of Isaiah 58, whose essence is found in verses 6–7:

Is not this the fast that I choose: to loose the bonds of wickedness, to undo the thongs of the yoke, to let the oppressed go free, and to break every yoke? Is it not to share your bread with the hungry, and bring the homeless poor into your house; when you see the naked, to cover him, and not to hide yourself from your own flesh?

(Isa 58:6–7)

Jesus is pushing against the perception that we find at Qumran and elsewhere, namely, that one group of Jews would be blessed, and the other destroyed. The thrust of his message resonates with the story of another *hasid* who lived before Jesus, Honi (Gr. Onias) the Circle Drawer.[60] Josephus recounts the story of his death. It occurs during the Hasmonean period, when the sons of Alexander Yannai (Jannaeus) and Shelomtzion (Salome) Alexandra, Hyrcanus and Aristobulus II vied for the throne. During Passover, as Aristobulus was held up in the temple due to Hyrcanus' support from King Aretas III, ruler of the Nabateans, Honi—described as a righteous man and beloved of God—was brought to Hyrcanus' camp. Knowing full well that God listened diligently to his prayers, he asked that Honi pray a curse on Aristobulus. Essentially, Honi was told by Hyrcanus, a Jewish leader, to curse a fellow Jew—his brother(!)—Aristobulus. Honi responded,

O God, the king of the whole world! Since those that stand now with me are your people, and those that are besieged are also your priests, I beseech you, that you will neither hearken to the prayers of those against these, nor bring to effect what these pray against those.

(Ant. 4:24)

The prayer would be Honi's last. When finished, he was immediately stoned by the Jews who were present. This is strikingly similar to the end of the Lukan narrative, except that Jesus survives: "When they heard this, all in the synagogue were filled with wrath. And they rose up and put him out of the city, and led him to the brow of the hill on which their city was built, that they might throw him down headlong" (Luke 4:28–29). Compared to Honi, Jesus' message was even more pointed. Not only did he highlight the misguided judgment of one Jewish community hoping for the harm or destruction of another—as in Josephus—he inserted Isaiah 58 to present a deeper challenge by suggesting that the "day of the Lord"—the time of his favor—is attained by feeding the hungry, clothing the naked, and providing a home for the homeless. In that sense, Jesus' statement, "today this scripture has been fulfilled in your hearing" (Luke 4:21), is not a self-proclamation of his own messianic self-awareness, but the affirmation that merciful and righteous actions—those matters that identify his movement—are what brings forth the time of God's favor.

CHARITY, DEEDS OF RECIPROCAL KINDNESS, AND THE IMAGE OF GOD IN THE GOSPELS

The Gospels were compiled during a transition period. After the destruction of the temple in AD 70 there appears to be a smaller amount of literature produced than before. This paucity of textual sources immediately after the destruction of the temple makes it difficult to assess how Judaism evolved between AD 70 and the codification of the Mishnah in AD 200. While the Mishnah legendarily claims a direct link of oral traditions back to Sinai (*m. Avot* 1), the reality is far more complex, and this direct link does not address them. Because of the Gospels' unique perspective, they offer additional information of the evolution of Judaism during this transition.

Some of the best examples of this are Jesus' teachings on charity, deeds of reciprocal kindness (*gemilut hasadim*),[61] and the "image of God." In the Second Temple period, prior to the time depicted in the Gospels, there was a new sensitivity that took hold within certain Jewish circles which elevated in importance some of the altruistic commandments in Leviticus (19:9, 10, 18, 34; 23:22) and Deuteronomy (14:28–29; 24:19, 21; 26:12–13), especially those regarding charity, loving one's neighbor, and the foreigner. As David Flusser notes, these ideas are attested in texts like the following,[62]

Anger and wrath, these also are abominations, and the sinful man will possess them. He that takes vengeance will suffer vengeance from the Lord, and he will firmly establish his sins. Forgive your neighbor the wrong he has done, and then your sins will be pardoned when you pray. Does a man harbor anger against another, and yet seek for healing from the Lord? Does he have no mercy toward a man like himself, and yet pray for his own sins? If he himself, being flesh, maintains wrath, who will make expiation for his sins? Remember the end of your life, and cease from enmity, remember destruction and death, and be true to the commandments. Remember the commandments, and do not be angry with your neighbor; remember the covenant of the Most High, and overlook ignorance.

(Sir 27:30–28:7)

By Jesus' day, loving your fellow man (Lev 19:18) became an essential expression of Jewish piety. The Levitical commandment is seen as an encapsulation of Jewish faith in the first century and is echoed by Hillel, in the aforementioned, Talmudic story about a potential convert. Asking for the entire Torah to be explained while he stood on one foot sets the challenge for both rabbis (*b. Shabb.* 31a). The *zugot* (pair), Hillel and Shammai, differ significantly, in that Shammai does not comply perceiving the challenge to be ridiculous. However, Hillel replies to the

The Siege and Destruction of Jerusalem by the Romans Under the Command of Titus, AD 70, *by David Roberts, 1850.*

Jewish Mother by Boris Schatz, 1929 (Yeshiva University Collection).

potential convert, "love your neighbor as yourself, the rest is commentary." For Flusser, altruistic social love achieved the "highest value index" by being considered the very essence of Judaism during the days of the Second Temple.[63]

Indeed, Jewish sources from this period begin to emphasize the importance of charity, almsgiving, and generally caring for the poor: "For charity delivers from death and keeps you from entering the darkness; and for all who practice it, charity is an excellent offering in the presence of the Most High" (Tob 4:10–11). Regarding the poor, the *Testament of Issachar* reads, "But love the Lord and your neighbor, have compassion on the poor and weak." But, while Tobit and the *Testaments of the Twelve Patriarchs*—of which the *Testament of Issachar* is part—highlight charity's growing importance, there is little that parallels the priority that charity receives among the rabbis. It is in the Tosefta that one reads, "charity and deeds of reciprocal kindness outweigh all the commandments in the Torah" (*t. Pe'ah* 4:19; also, *b. Bava Batra* 9a; *b. Sukkah* 49b).[64] In later midrashim, charity comes to be known as *ha-mitzvah*, "the commandment" (e.g., *Lev. Rab.* § 34). This transition of charity and deeds of reciprocal kindness from increasing importance in Jewish practice of the first century to one that takes priority over other commandments is not witnessed in texts outside of the Gospels. The Gospels alone are a witness to this subtle, yet complex, shift.

The Story of the Rich Young Man. First, it should be noted that charity is depicted in the Gospels as a point of *halakhah*, that is, Torah observance. Scholars often treat it as one of Jesus' ethical priorities but in Judaism ethics, as we have noted, are not separate from the other parts of the Jewish law. Jesus speaks about charity—along with other commandments—in the pericope of "The Rich Young Man."

Matthew 19:16–22	Mark 10:17–22	Luke 18:18–23
16 And behold, one came up to him, saying, "Teacher, what good deed must I do, to have eternal life?" 17 And he said to him, "Why do you ask me about what is good? One there is who is good. If you would enter life, keep the commandments." 18 He said to him, "Which?" And Jesus said, "You shall not kill, You shall not commit adultery, You shall not steal, You shall not bear false witness, 19 Honor your father and mother, and, You shall love your neighbor as yourself." 20 The young man said to him, "All these I have observed; what do I still lack?" 21 Jesus said to him, "If you would be perfect, go, sell what you possess and give to the poor, and you will have treasure in heaven; and come, follow me." 22 When the young man heard this he went away sorrowful; for he had great possessions.	17 And as he was setting out on his journey, a man ran up and knelt before him, and asked him, "Good Teacher, what must I do to inherit eternal life?" 18 And Jesus said to him, "Why do you call me good? No one is good but God alone. 19 You know the commandments: 'Do not kill, Do not commit adultery, Do not steal, Do not bear false witness, Do not defraud, Honor your father and mother.'" 20 And he said to him, "Teacher, all these I have observed from my youth." 21 And Jesus looking upon him loved him, and said to him, "You lack one thing; go, sell what you have, and give to the poor, and you will have treasure in heaven; and come, follow me." 22 At that saying his countenance fell, and he went away sorrowful; for he had great possessions.	18 And a ruler asked him, "Good Teacher, what shall I do to inherit eternal life?" 19 And Jesus said to him, "Why do you call me good? No one is good but God alone. 20 You know the commandments: 'Do not commit adultery, Do not kill, Do not steal, Do not bear false witness, Honor your father and mother.'" 21 And he said, "All these I have observed from my youth." 22 And when Jesus heard it, he said to him, "One thing you still lack. Sell all that you have and distribute to the poor, and you will have treasure in heaven; and come, follow me." 23 But when he heard this he became sad, for he was very rich.

The Matthean version especially notes the legal nature of the conversation, "And he said to him, 'If you would enter life, keep the commandments'" (Matt 19:17). More importantly, the account shows the priority of charity with Jesus' instruction to the rich man to sell his possessions and give to the poor. It betrays Jesus' opinion regarding charity. The Lukan version, in particular, heightens this perspective by adding that the young man is to "sell all" (*panta poleison*: πάντα...πώλησον; Luke 18:22). This prioritization is highlighted when the Gospels are compared with two lists preserved in the Mishnah and Tosefta. Both lists are part of larger conversations regarding which deeds accrue reward and punishment in this world, and principal in the world to come. The list in the Mishnah and Tosefta make known that the final item on each list takes priority over the rest. So too, it appears that Jesus' final point, to give to the poor,[65] takes priority over the rest.

"The Rich Ruler"	Mishnah/Tosefta *Pe'ah*
Jesus' Response: Deeds in order to inherit eternal life	Deeds to which one receives punishment in this world and principal in the world to come
• Do not kill • Do not commit adultery • Do not steal • Do not bear false witness	• Idolatry • Sexual Immorality • Murder (T) • Sexual immorality (T) • Slander[66]
	Deeds to which one receives reward in this world and principal in the world to come
• Honor father and mother • Love your neighbor as yourself • Give to the poor	• Honor father and mother (M) • Making peace with your fellow man (M) • 1. Deeds of loving-kindness (M) • 2. Doing good [related to the righteous person] (T)

The same association between deed and reward, specifically deeds of reciprocal kindness, appears in the pericope of the "The Last Judgment" (Matt 25:31–46). The scene is completely eschatological: the Son of Man sits on a glorious throne to judge the nations. All of humanity is envisioned as sheep and goats, which the Son of Man separates "as a shepherd" (v. 32). The goats are placed on the left side of the throne, the sheep on the right side. The former goes away to eternal punishment, while the latter, the righteous, are rewarded with eternal life (v. 46). The reward and punishment in this pericope revolve around deeds of reciprocal kindness (what the rabbis called "*gemilut hasadim*"):

> Then the King will say to those at his right hand, "Come, O blessed of my Father, inherit the kingdom prepared for you from the foundation of the world; for I was hungry and you gave me food, I was thirsty and you gave me drink, I was a stranger and you welcomed me, I was naked and you clothed me, I was sick and you visited me, I was in prison and you came to me." Then the righteous will answer

> him, "Lord, when did we see thee hungry and feed thee, or thirsty and give thee drink? And when did we see thee a stranger and welcome thee, or naked and clothe thee? And when did we see thee sick or in prison and visit thee?"
>
> (Matt 25:35–39)

The ruinous end for the goats and glorious reward for the righteous, bring us back to the Levitical neighbor-loving command.

Charity and the Image of God. But why must we love our neighbor and be actively merciful to those in need? The answer revolves around ancient Jewish views of humanity, which varied. Loving one's neighbor is based on the notion that every person is created in the "image of God" (*tselem elohim*: צֶלֶם אֱלֹהִים, Gen 1:27). But this is only one of multiple opinions. One finds in the Thanksgiving Hymns of Qumran multiple descriptions of humanity as "creatures of clay and dust" (*yetzer afar; yetzer homer*: יצר עפר; יצר חמר), in part a modification of Gen 2, which intentionally debases human existence as utterly inferior and valueless.[67] Elsewhere the *yaḥad* of Qumran describes humanity as "mere spit" (1QHa 20:35), "so much spit, mere nipped off clay" (1QS 11:21–22), and a "foundation of shame and a spring of filth" (1QHa 9:24). This further betrays the justification for the Qumran community to command its members to "hate" all outsiders. On the other hand, the neighbor-loving command is found in other sources, where the *imago dei* is utilized to speak of humanity's innate importance (Sir 17:1–4; see also Wis 2:23) and ability of every person to follow God's commandments. Humanity's highest valuation, uttered by Rabbi Akiva, also revolves around the divine image, "Precious is the human being, who was created in the image [of God]" (*Avot* 3:14). Thus, the reason to love the "other" is because he/she bears the image of the king and, as a result, every person is inherently valuable and completely deserving of merciful care when there is need.

Along with Matthew 25, the concept of deed and reward, and the divine image, continually support the Gospels' teaching that actions, or lack thereof, towards your neighbor have personal ramifications: "Judge not, that you be not judged. For with the judgment you pronounce you will be judged, and the measure you give will be the measure you get" (Matt 7:1–2); "For if you forgive men their trespasses, your heavenly Father also will forgive you; but if you do not forgive men their trespasses, neither will your Father forgive your trespasses" (Matt 6:14–15). The relationship between God and humanity portrayed here is triangular.[68] The manner in which you love, judge, or trespass against your neighbor, namely, another person created in the image of God, establishes a measurement by which God will judge you. Often, the best indicator of what one truly thinks about God is how they will treat another. Belief that everyone is stamped with the image of the king—inherently valuable, regardless of socio-economic, or religious standing—is the driving force behind being kind and merciful to all. But it is also more than that.

Tribute to Caesar and the Image of God. The idea of the divine image appears again in the account "On Paying Tribute to Caesar" (Matt 22:15–22/Mark 12:13–17/Luke 20:20–26) where Jesus is questioned whether it is appropriate to pay taxes to the Roman Emperor. His response hinges on utilizing the image on the coin used to pay taxes in contrast to God's image. After requesting to see a coin, he asks the audience, "Whose likeness and inscription is on the coin?" The response of the audience tells us that it is Caesar's image. The coin that the Gospels are referring to bear the face of Tiberius with an inscription that reads, *Tiberius Augustus divi Augusti filius Augustus*.[69] Jesus' reply is simple, yet profound: "Then render to Caesar the things that are Caesar's, and to God the things that are God's" (Luke 20:25). It answers both questions deftly, first, pay your taxes and, second, remember whose image is impressed upon you and give that to God.

Of course, giving to God is abstract. How does one give to the Almighty? Unfortunately, none of the Gospels go on to explain what is meant by giving to God, though we have an implication of the divine image. There are two points that may give us some understanding. First, as discussed above, the "Judgment of the Nations" scene in Matthew 25 pivots on the "image of God." The King's response that he was thirsty, hungry, imprisoned, and sick cause the righteous to ask, "Lord, when did we see thee hungry and feed thee, or thirsty and give thee drink? And when did we see thee a stranger and welcome thee, or naked and clothe thee? And when did we see thee sick or in prison and visit thee?" (Matt 25:37–39). The response is said to come from the King and not the Son of Man, "And the King will answer them, 'Truly, I say to you, as you did it to one of the least of these my brethren, you did it to me'" (Matt 25:40). Often in Jewish literature, the king is representative of God. The correlation between those in need—the least of these—and the king, is the image of God and the resulting triangular relationship with God. Therefore, the manner in which the righteous act towards their neighbor, brother, sister, foreigner etc., is not only effectual to those receiving, but it is as if the same has been done to the Almighty (see *b. Shabb.* 151b). Indeed, the lack of action bears the same ramifications; for example, not giving water to the thirsty would be equal to neglecting God. Second, are references to laying up "treasure in heaven" (Matt 19:16–22/Mark 10:17–22/Luke 18:18–23; Matt 6:20; Luke 12:33)?[70] In the Second

Denarius coin of Tiberius Caesar (courtesy York Museums Trust, Yorkshire Museum).

(above, obv.) Laureated Caesar with inscription that reads TI[BERIUS] CAESAR DIVI AVG[VSTI] F[ILIUS] AVGVSTVS.

(below, rev.) Female seated, holding sceptre and branch, with inscription PONTIF[EX] MAXIM[US].

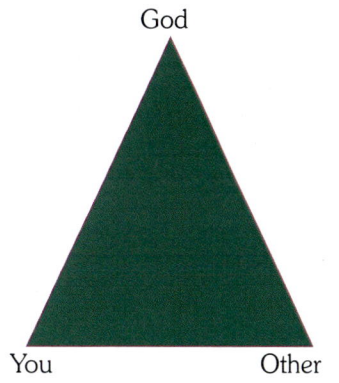

(left) The triangular relationship with God (see endnote 68).

Temple period, this idiom always means the giving of alms (Tob 4:9–10, 12:8; Sir 29:11–12; *T. Levi* 13:5; *2 Enoch* 50:5). With charity, one makes a deposit in the heavens where it cannot deteriorate. It is essentially giving to God and securing oneself a place in the world to come. In light of this, Jesus' response where he invokes the "image of God," in contrast to the Tiberius coin, again reminds his audience of the importance to taking care of those in need. While the "On Paying Tribute to Caesar" account does not specify how one is to give to God, the Gospels' general elevation of charity that we see elsewhere among the rabbis (*t. Pe'ah* 4:19)—and the Levitical command to love one's neighbor (and foreigner; see above)—both of which are apparently founded on the concept that all of humanity bears the divine image, makes sense of "give to God what is God's." The unspoken message, which reverberates throughout Jewish society in the first century, is that giving to God can only be accomplished by caring and being merciful to your neighbor, the poor, and the needy.

The growing importance of the neighborly-loving commandment (Lev 19:18—even 19:34), charity, and deeds of reciprocal kindness, is already seen in first-century sources outside of the Bible. The manner in which they all reach their pinnacle in rabbinic literature is a process for which there is a scarcity of witnesses.[71] The Gospels are in a unique position to be a source for ancient Judaism, where there would otherwise be none. Often, when they preserve traditions—which first appear on the lips of specific rabbis and date to the later, post-Second Temple period (e.g., the kingdom of God/heaven)—they offer a snapshot, depicting the transition and evolution of Judaism. Futhermore, it may indicate that these ideas predate the temple's destruction. Indeed, the dating of these texts (e.g., Gospels, DSS, etc.), establish a linear, historical development where one is forced to speak of a transition, or shift, in the Jewish world. However, it should be noted that the evolution of religious thought is never so neat or linear. In regard to loving your neighbor, charity, deeds of reciprocal kindness, and the image of God, the Gospels fill in a lacuna in their transition from growing importance to becoming the highest index of Jewish piety.

THE GOSPELS AS THE FIRST LITERARY WITNESS TO JEWISH PRACTICE

The Gospels are part of a formative period in the history of Judaism. Scholars have yet to wholly appreciate that they are, at times, the first literary witnesses to Jewish practice that is only referenced again in much later Jewish literature, or present narratives of communities participating in specific Jewish events (e.g., a Passover meal; visiting synagogue on the Sabbath) that are only referenced in contemporary sources.

The Birth, Naming, and Circumcision of Saint John the Baptist *by Giovanni Baronzio, 1335.*

Naming on the Eighth Day. In the late 1980s, the rabbinic scholar Shmuel Safrai noted that the tradition of naming a son on the eighth day after a son's birth—the day of his circumcision—is mentioned for the first time in Jewish history in Luke,[72]

Now the time came for Elizabeth to be delivered, and she gave birth to a son.... And on the eighth day they came to circumcise the child; and they would have named him Zechariah after his father, but his mother said, "Not so; he shall be called John." And they said to her, "None of your kindred is called by this name."

(Luke 1:57, 59–60)

And at the end of eight days, when he was circumcised, he was called Jesus, the name given by the angel before he was conceived in the womb.

(Luke 2:21)

Both John and Jesus are named on the eighth day. The tradition, which is now practiced in many Jewish communities, originates in the Second Temple period. The first reference to this tradition, outside of the Gospels, appears in a 7th-century rabbinic work, *Pirke de-Rabbi Eliezer*, "The parents of Moses saw that his appearance was like that of an angel of God. They circumcised him on the eighth day and called him Yekutiel" (48). The other Gospels make no mention of the naming of either John or Jesus, indicating that Luke has access to an independent, Jewish source that is not in need of Mark or, the hypothetical synoptic source, *Q(uelle)*.

Abraham's Bosom. In the so-called Parable of the Rich Man and Lazarus (Luke 16:19–31), Lazarus, the poor man who lays at the rich man's gate, dies. Upon his death, Luke states that he is "carried by angels to Abraham's bosom" (*tou kolpon Abraam*: τὸν κόλπον Ἀβραάμ). The rich man, having received good during his lifetime, is in Hades and in torment. Seeing Lazarus in the bosom, the rich man requests that something merciful be done on his behalf, "Father Abraham, have mercy upon me, and send Lazarus to dip the end of his finger in water and cool my tongue; for I am in anguish in this flame" (v. 24). The reference to Abraham's bosom appears to refer to a postmortem paradise, heaven, or, in the parlance of the rabbis, some version of the world to come (*olam ha-ba*). In Jewish sources, Abraham, and the other patriarchs, are associated with the afterlife (see 4 Macc 13:17; also Matt 8:11; *Gen. Rab.* 48:8), but there are no references to "Abraham's Bosom." The earliest reference appears in the 7th-century midrash *Peskita de-Rav Kahana*, in an interpretation attributed to R. Judah ben Goriah on Psalm 79:12, "Return sevenfold into the bosom (*heikam*: חֵיקָם) of our neighbors, the taunts with which they have taunted you, O Lord!," which is understood as a memorial against the wicked Amalekites because of what Amalek had done to Israelites who were now in "Abraham's bosom" (*be-heiko shel Abraham*: בחיקו של אברהם; 3:6). The same meaning appears in the 8th-century Babylonian Talmud (*Qidd.* 71b–72a) and the 9th-century midrash, *Pesikta Rabbati* (43). Furthermore, it is unlikely Luke's is a late editorial addition by a scribe since "Abraham's bosom" appears in very early manuscripts that predate these *midrashim*.

The Reading of the *Haftarah*. Scholars have noted that the reading of Isaiah in the synagogue at Nazareth (Luke 4:16–19) is the earliest evidence for the reading of the *haftarah*.[73] The *haftarah* is a reading from the prophetic portion of the Bible that is read after the Torah portion. It was read on Sabbaths, festivals, and on particular fast days. Fishbane notes that in a medieval legend the reading of the *haftarah* commenced under the persecutions of Antiochus IV Epiphanes, but that the lack of ancient sources makes its origins unclear. Luke describes it as a common synagogal practice by the time of Jesus, since the reading of Isaiah itself seems largely unremarkable to the Evangelist.

Preservation of Life[74] (*pikuach nefesh*). One of the most important principles in Judaism is the "preservation of life" (*pikuach nefesh*: פיקוח נפש). All commandments, except for the prohibitions against murder, idolatry, and unchastity, are set aside on the Sabbath to save a life that is in danger.[75] The first explicit reference of this principle occurs in the *Mekhilta de-Rabbi Ishmael*. Arguing for the importance of the preservation of life in light of other commandments,

> R. Simon b. Mensaya says: The duty of saving life (פיקוח נפש) should supersede the Sabbath laws, and the following reasoning favors it: If the punishing

Reading the Torah (photo גמלאי עירייה טבריה via Wikimedia Commons).

> of murder sets aside the Temple service, which has precedence over the Sabbath, how much the more should the duty of saving life, which likewise sets aside the Temple service, supersede the Sabbath law.
> (*Nezikin* 4 on Exod 21:12–14)[76]

Yet, the importance of an individual life is already mentioned earlier in the Mishnah, "Therefore man was created alone, to teach you that whoever destroys a single life is deemed by Scripture as if he had destroyed a whole world. And whoever saves a single soul is deemed by Scripture as if he had saved a whole world" (*m. Sanh.* 4:5). This is likely related to the Akivan statement, "precious is the human being, who was created in the image" (*m. Avot* 3:14). In that sense, each human life is inherently valuable. While this principle likely exists in an early period, it appears that Luke is the first text to mention the importance of saving life, even on the Sabbath.[77]

> On another sabbath, when he entered the synagogue and taught, a man was there whose right hand was withered. And the scribes and the Pharisees watched him, to see whether he would heal on the sabbath, so that they might find an accusation against him. But he knew their thoughts, and he said to the man who had the withered hand, "Come and stand here." And he rose and stood there. And Jesus said to them, "I ask you, is it lawful on the sabbath to do good or to do harm, to save life or to destroy it?" And he looked around on them all, and said to him, "Stretch out your hand." And he did so, and his hand was restored. But they were filled with fury and discussed with one another what they might do to Jesus.
> (Luke 6:6–11)

The implication in Luke is obvious, the "preservation of life" supersedes the Sabbath. Some have connected the origins of *pikuach nefesh* with the account in 1 Macc 2:27–48 where Mattathias decides that they would fight on the Sabbath so that "they would not all die as other Jews had died in the caves." There still remains some question as to whether self-preservation is one and the same with the preservation of another person's life.

Ritual fringes (Heb. tzitzit) (photo Yair Aronshtam, via Wikimedia Commons).

Ritual Fringes (*tzitzit*). There remains a question as to how pervasive the wearing of ritual fringes was in Jewish society. Despite having the fringes mentioned in the Torah (Num 15:38; Deut 22:12), there are no Second Temple sources, outside of the New Testament, that refer to their use. The Gospels use the Greek term *kraspedon* (κράσπεδον)—the Septuagintal translation for these ritual fringes (*tzitzit*: צִיצִת)—to describe the fringes that Jesus wore and the manner in which some found healing (Matt 9:20/Luke 8:44; Matt 14:36/Mark 6:56). The Pharisees are also spoken of as wearing them (Matt 23:5). It may be that the wearing of these fringes were done by those with a particular observance to the commandments in Numbers and Deuteronomy. The next reference to *tzitzit* is not until the 3rd century AD, in the Tannaitic halakhic *midrashim* (*Mek. R. Ish. Shir.* 3 to Exod 15:2; *Sif. Num.* 115:1).

Attendance of Synagogue on the Sabbath. It is common practice in Judaism to visit synagogue on the Sabbath. The prevalent practice among Jewish communities in the first century made explicit references to it unnecessary. Evidence of such a service appears in the Mishnah (*m. Sukk.* 3:13). Yet, the first literary witness of a Jewish person going to synagogue on the Sabbath appears in Mark (1:21, 6:2) and Luke (6:6, 13:14). Luke, in particular, notes that Jesus' visit was a "custom" (*to eiothos*: τὸ εἰωθός; Luke 4:16).

Narration of Passover Pre–70 Meal. The celebration of Passover in the Second Temple period is spoken about by Philo (*Spec. Laws* B, 145) and Josephus (*Ant.* 3:248–251).[78]

Jewish pilgrims on their way to the Western Wall during Sukkot (Feast of Tabernacles) (photo Israel Government Press Office).

First-century synagogue at Masada (photo Oren Rozen, via Wikimedia Commons).

Josephus, in particular, attests to the eating of the Passover sacrifice as groups, families, etc. (*Ant.* 3:248). Additionally, there are an abundant number of occasions in rabbinic literature where it is clear that the lamb is roasted and eaten in the home (e.g., *m. Ta'an.* 3:8). Accounts narrating such a meal, however, are altogether missing in Jesus' day, despite the existence of such events. Matthew's, Mark's, and Luke's description of the Last Supper is the first narration of people eating such a meal in the history of Judaism—John's meal occurs before the Passover (13:1). Although, the earliest forms of these meals appear to be different than what eventually evolves into the *Seder* meal after the destruction of the Temple. These pre-rabbinic meals included the sacrifice and the recitation of the *Hallel* (Pss 113–118). Luke, of the three Evangelists, reflects the order of the meal that was standard Jewish practice, the blessing of the wine (*cos rishon*: כוס ראשון) and then the bread. While the Last Supper is not technically a *Seder*, it is a narration of a pre-Rabbinic Passover meal that we do not find in other Second Temple sources.

Narration of Jewish Pilgrimage. Pilgrimage was another common practice in the first century. While Josephus speaks of pilgrimages (Passover—In the time of Josiah, *Ant.* 10:68–73; Second Temple: *Ant.* 14:25–28, 17:213–215, 18:29, 20:106; *War* 2:210, 242; Pentecost—*Ant.* 14:337, 17:254; *War* 1:253, 2:42; Sukkot—*Ant.* 11:77, 13:371), the Gospels are the first to narrate particular Jews visiting Jerusalem during these feasts (Luke 2; 22:7). Among the Jews observing pilgrimages are Mary and Joseph, about whom Luke describes as going to Jerusalem "every year" on the Passover. Jesus seems to follow this custom, not only during his Passion week, but also at other times in his ministry (John 2:23). He is also depicted visiting Jerusalem on non-pilgrimage feast days like Hanukkah ("Feast of Dedication," John 10:22). Moreover, in Acts 2, both Peter and the disciples are present in Jerusalem for Pentecost/Shavuot (Feast of Weeks)—another pilgrimage feast—as are Jews from all over the Mediterranean. Paul himself makes his way to Jerusalem, sailing by Ephesus, to observe Pentecost (Acts 20:16).

NOTES AND REFERENCES

1. Joseph Klausner, *Yeshu ha-Notzri: Zemano, Chayav, ve-Torato* (Jerusalem, 1926 [Hebrew]); idem, *Jesus of Nazareth: His Life, Times, and Teaching* (trans. Herbert Danby; New York: Macmillan, 1945); David Flusser, *Jesus in Selbstzeugnissen u. Bilddokumenten* (Reinbek bei Hamburg: Rowohlt, 1968); See esp. updated editions, David Flusser and R. Steven Notley, *Jesus* (3rd ed.; Jerusalem: Magnes Press, 2001); idem, *The Sage from Galilee: Rediscovering Jesus' Genius* (Grand Rapids; Eerdmans, 2007); Hebrew translation, *Yeshu* (Jerusalem: Magnes Press and Dvir, 2012); Shalom ben Chorin, *Bruder Jesus; der Nazarener in Jüdischer Sicht* (München, 1967); idem, *Brother Jesus: The Nazarene through Jewish Eyes* (trans. Jared Stephen Klein; Athens; London; University of Georgia Press. 2001). Often the Third Quest, and all quests, for that matter, had little to do with carving out an image of a historical persona, but rather betrayed scholars' assumptions regarding the nature of the Gospels, Matthew, Mark, Luke, and John.

2. To the extent that the Gospels have preserved traditions from a much later, non-Jewish context, remains a matter of debate. This is complicated by how one defines "non-Jewish." Surely, the influence of Classical Greek works like Aesop's Fables in the Gospels does not indicate a departure from Judaism but is an indication of the complex cultural matrix that was Second Temple Judaism.

3. Although subsequent parallels with later Amoraic texts are evident as well.

4. Kristin Romey, "The Real Story Behind the 'House of Jesus' Apostles' Discovery, *National Geographic*, http://news.nationalgeographic.com/2017/08/jesus-bible-apostles-bethsaida-israel-archaeology/, August 7th 2017.

5. Indeed, collections of Jewish Pseudepigrapha do not agree in content because "Pseudepigrapha" is not an ancient compilation. The most well known are *The Apocrypha and Pseudepigrapha of the Old Testament* (2 vols., ed. R. H. Charles; Clarendon: Oxford University Press, 1913); *The Old Testament Pseudepigrapha* (2 vols., ed. James Charlesworth; New York: Doubleday, 1983); More recently, *Old Testament Pseudepigrapha: More Non-Canonical Scriptures* (ed., Richard Bauckham; James Davila et al.; Grand Rapids: Eerdmans, 2013).

6. Frank Moore Cross, *The Ancient Library of Qumran* (3rd ed., Minneapolis: Fortress Press, 1995).

7. "Midrash" comes from the verb *darash*, "to search."

8. E.g., see *The New Testament and Rabbinic Literature* (ed. R. Bierunger, F. García-Martínez et al.; Leiden: Brill, 2010); R. Steven Notley and Jeffrey P. García, "Hebrew Only-Exegesis: A Philological Approach to Jesus' Use of the Hebrew Bible," in *The Language Environment of First Century Judaea: Jerusalem Studies in the Synoptic Gospels*, vol. 2, JCP 26 (Leiden: Brill), 348–374; Jeffrey P. García, "'What Do I Still Lack?' Jesus, Charity, and the Early Rabbis," in *The Gospels in First-Century Judaea Proceedings of the Inaugural Conference of Nyack College's Graduate Program in Ancient Judaism and Christian Origins, August 29th, 2013*, eds. R. Steven Notley and J. P. García (Leiden: Brill, 2015), 20–43.

9. Nazareth is first mentioned by Sextus Iulius Africanus, in Ep. Arist. (2nd–3rd cent. AD). See Yoram Tsafrir, Leah Di Segni, Judith Green, *Tabula Imperii Romani: Iudaea, Palaestina—Maps and Gazetteer* (Jerusalem: the Israel Academy of Sciences and Humanities, 1994), 194–195.

10. Anson F. Rainey and R. Steven Notley, *The Sacred Bridge* (Jerusalem: Carta, 2005), 350–351.

11. This was pointed out to me by Marc Turnage in a private conversation.

12. Mordechai Aviam, "Border between Jews and Gentiles in the Galilee" in *Jews, Pagans, and Christians in the Galilee—35 Years of Archeological Excavations and Surveys: Hellenistic to Byzantine Period* (Rochester: University of Rochester Press, 2004), 9–21.

13. Contra R. T. France, *The Gospel of Matthew* (NICNT; Grand Rapids: Eerdmans, 2007). See Mark Chancey, *The Myth of the Gentile Galilee*; Jeffrey P. García, "Jesus the Galilean, a Stranger in Judea?," *Jerusalem Perspective*, [https://www.jerusalemperspective.com/12154/; accessed: June 13th, 2017].

14. Both are also the only Gospel texts with birth narratives.

15. Rainey and Notley, *The Sacred Bridge*, 349–350.

16. Rainey and Notley, *The Sacred Bridge*, 349–350.

17. Marc Turnage, "The Census of Quirinius and Luke 2," in *Windows Into the Bible: Cultural and Historical Insights from the Bible for Modern Readers* (Springfield, Mo: Logion Press, 2016), 157–165.

18. Named Caesarea in AD 14 by Philip, Herod the Great's son, and Philippi in order to distinguish it from Ceasarea, the coastal city.

19. *Ant.* 17:317–320; see Rainey and Notley, *The Sacred Bridge*, 348.

20. This was noted to me in a private conversation by Marc Turnage.

21. R. Steven Notley, "Pontius Pilate: Sadist or Saint," *BAR* 43/4 (2017): 40–60.

22. Yochanan Breuer states, "Scholars had been of the opinion that, after the return of the Babylonian exiles, Hebrew no longer served as a spoken language. On this account, Hebrew retained its status as a holy tongue and was used in prayer and in Torah study, and for this reason the Mishnah and contemporary tannaitic literature was composed in Hebrew, but in everyday life Aramaic alone was spoken. Today this view is no longer accepted, the scholarly consensus now being that Hebrew speech survived in all walks of life at least until the end of the Tannaitic period (the beginning of the third century AD), from "Aramaic in Late Antiquity," in *The Cambridge History of Judaism* vol. 4: *The Late Roman-Rabbinic Period*, ed. S. Katz (Cambridge: Cambridge University Press, 2006), 457–458. See also, Kutscher, *A History of the Hebrew Language*, 117–118; and R. Steven Notley and Jeffrey P. García, "The Hebrew Scriptures in the Third Gospel," in *Searching the Scriptures: Studies in Context and Intertextuality*, ed. Craig A. Evans and Jeremiah J. Johnston (New York; London: Bloomsbury T&T Clark, 2015), 128–130.

23. See R. Steven Notley, "Non-Septuagintal Hebraisms in the Third Gospel: An Inconvenient Truth," in *The Language Environment*, 320–346.

24. Raphael Posner, "Charity," in *Encyclopedia Judaica*, ed. F. Skolnik and M. Birnbaum; 22 vols; 2nd ed. (Detroit: Macmillan Reference USA; Jerusalem: Keter Publishing Ltd.; 2007), 4:569–571; also, E.P. Sanders, "Charity and Love," in *Judaism: Practice and Belief 63 B.C.E–66 C.E.* (London: SCM Press; Philadelphia: Trinity International Press, 2005), 230–235.

25. Stephen C. Carlson, "The Accommodations of Joseph and Mary in Bethlehem: *Kataluma* in Luke 2.7," *NTS* (56): 326–342. See also, Marc Turnage, "The Birth of Jesus" in *Windows*, 222–230.

26. David Flusser, "A Comment on the Prayer for the Welfare of King Jonathan," *Tarbiz* 61 (1992): 297–300 [Heb.]; translated and reprinted in *Judaism of the Second Temple Period*, vol. 1: *Qumran and Apocalypticism*, trans. Azzan Yadin (Grand Rapids: Eerdmans; Jerusalem: Magnes Press; Jerusalem: Jerusalem Perspective, 2007), 170–174.

27. Shmuel Safrai, *Jesus and the Hasidim*, https://www.jerusalemperspective.com/2685/ [www.Jerusalemperspective.com; Accessed: July 24th 2017]; idem, "Teaching Pietists in Mishnaic Literature," *JJS* 16 (1965): 15–33.

28. Lawrence Schiffman, *Halakhah at Qumran* (Leiden: Brill, 1975); *Reclaiming the Dead Sea Scrolls*; ABRL (New York: Doubleday, 1994), 63–158.

29. Despite the requirement for living water in the *mikva'ot*, the Mishnah provides regulations for the amount fresh, hand-drawn water that can be added to the *miqva'ot* and still allow the water to be used for ritual immersions.

30. Technically, in the Hebrew Bible God finishes his work *on* the seventh day: "And God finished his work, which he made, on the seventh day; and he rested on the seventh day" (וַיְכַל אֱלֹהִים בַּיּוֹם הַשְּׁבִיעִי מְלַאכְתּוֹ אֲשֶׁר עָשָׂה וַיִּשְׁבֹּת בַּיּוֹם הַשְּׁבִיעִי; Gen 2:2). Both the Samaritan Pentateuch and the Septuagint, sensing some tension, alter the text to conform with complete rest on the seventh day. The Samaritan Pentateuch reads that God finished his work on the sixth day (הששי) and rested on the seventh (השביעי). The LXX similarly reads, "And God finished on the sixth day his works which he made, and he ceased on the seventh day" (καὶ συνετέλεσεν ὁ θεὸς ἐν τῇ ἡμέρᾳ τῇ ἕκτῃ τὰ ἔργα αὐτοῦ, ἃ ἐποίησεν, καὶ κατέπαυσεν τῇ ἡμέρᾳ τῇ ἑβδόμῃ).

31. Ander Runesson, *The Origins of the Synagogue: A Socio-Historical Study*, CBNTS 37 (Stockholm, Sweden: Almquist and Wiksell International, 2001), 478ff.

32. Although this is not the only name used for synagogues in the Diaspora (see Runesson, *The Origins*, 171–172).

33. Jeremy Penner, *Patterns of Daily Prayer in Second Temple Judaism*, STDJ 104 (Leiden: Brill, 2012), 70–71.

34. David Flusser, "Judaism in the Second Temple Period," in *Judaism of the Second Temple Period*, vol. 2: *The Jewish Sages and Their Literature*, trans. Azzan Yadin (Grand Rapids: Eerdmans; Jerusalem: Magnes Press; Jerusalem: Jerusalem Perspective, 2009), 6–43.

35. See Sidnie White Crawford's cautions about the use of this language in the New Testament ("Mothers, Sisters, and Elders: Titles from Women in Second Temple Jewish and early Christian Communities," in *The Dead Sea Scrolls as Background to Post-Biblical Judaism and Early Christianity*, ed. James R. Davila (Leiden: Brill, 2003], 177–191).

36. Tal Ilan, "Post-Biblical and Rabbinic Women," in *Jewish Women's Archive: Encylopedia* [https://jwa.org/encyclopedia/article/post-biblical-and-rabbinic-women/; accessed: July 25th, 2017].

37. See Shmuel Safrai and Zeev Safrai, *Haggadah of the Sages* (Jerusalem: Carta, 2007).

38. *Josephus: Jewish Antiquities*, vol. 6: Books 14–15, trans. H. St. Thackeray, LCL 242 (Cambridge, MA: Harvard University Press, 1930), 457–459.
39. Aristobulus I was the first to claim both but his rule lasted less than a year (104–103 BC).
40. Shmuel Safrai, ed., *Jewish People in the First Century*, vol. 2: *Historical Geography, Political History, Social, Cultural and Religious Life and Institutions*, CRINT 15 (Assen: Van Gorcum; Philadelphia: Fortress Press, 1987), 583–584.
41. Lester Grabbe, *Judaic Religion in the Second Temple Period: Belief and Practice from the Exile to Yavneh* (London and New York: Routledge, 2000), 135–137.
42. Jeffrey P. García, "'See My Hands and My Feet:' Shedding Light in a Johannine Midrash" in *John, Jesus, and History*, vol. 2: *Aspects of Historicity in the Fourth Gospel* (Atlanta: SBL, 2009), 325–334.
43. Martin Hengel, *Crucifixion* (London: SCM Press; Philadelphia: Fortress Press, 1977), 22–32.
44. Brad H. Young, *The Parables: Jewish Tradition and Christian Interpretation* (Hendrickson Publishers, 1998), 3.
45. Zeev Safrai and R. Steven Notley, *Parables of the Sages* (Jerusalem: Carta, 2011) 5–6.
46. Translation from Notley and Safrai, *Parables of the Sages*, 298 (par. no. 381a).
48. This was suggested to me in a private conversation with Steven Notley.
49. The term *halakhah* (הלכה) comes from the verb *halak* (הלך; "to walk") and is a rabbinic term that reflects aspects of observing the commandments.
50. Flusser and Notley, *The Sage*, 35.
51. For fuller treatments of this text, see Isaac W. Oliver, *Torah-Praxis after 70 CE*, WUNT 2 355 (Tübingen: Mohr Seibeck, 2013), 80–113; Thomas Kazen, *Scripture, Interpretation, and Authority?*, WUNT 320 (Tübingen: Mohr Seibeck, 2013), 53–112.
52. Lawrence H. Schiffman, *The Halakhah at Qumran*, 84–133.
53. Readers of Matthew's and Mark's versions will note that the references to David are slightly different. Moreover, 1 Samuel makes no mention whether the Davidic account occurs on the Sabbath, although this appears to be the understanding in later rabbinic tradition (*b. Menah.* 95b; *Yalq. Shim.* 130).
54. This is dependent on when one dates 4 Ezra, which preserves in chapter 8 a clear example of *qal v'homer*. Most scholars date this text to after the destruction of the temple in AD 70. The author refers to this example in "Creation, Composition, and Condition: On Being Human in Early Judaism" (unpublished dissertation, New York University), chap. 2.
55. A. M. Gale argues that this *middah* is utilized in Matt 12:1–8, in *Redefining Ancient Borders: The Jewish Scribal Framework of Matthew's Gospel* (London: T&T Clark International, 2005), 133–138.
56. Jeffrey P. García, "'Treasure in Heaven:' Examining an Ancient Idiom for Charity; *Jerusalem Perspective* [https://www.jerusalemperspective.com/12036/; accessed: July 28th, 2017]; also, Gary Anderson, "A Treasury in Heaven: The Exegesis of Proverbs 10:2 in the Second Temple Period" in *Hebrew Bible and Ancient Israel* 1/3 (2012: 351–367; idem, *Charity: The Place of the Poor in Biblical Tradition* (Connecticut: Yale University Press, 2014); Almut Hintze, "Treasure in Heaven: A Theme in Comparative Religion" in *Irano-Judaica VI: Studies Relating to Jewish Contacts with Persian Culture Throughout the Ages*, ed. Shaul Shaked and A. Netzer (Jerusalem: Ben-Zvi, 2008), 9–36.
57. This was first suggested to me in a conversation with Marc Turnage.
58. Turnage, "The Good Samaritan," in *Windows*, 369–384.
59. Shmuel Safrai, "Synagogue and Sabbath," *Jerusalem Perspective* 23 (November–December, 1989), 8–10; see also http://www.jerusalemperspective.com/2424/. Safrai also recognizes that Luke's report about Jesus reading alone is in accord with other ancient witnesses (e.g., *m. Sot.* 7.7–8; *m. Yoma* 7.1; Josephus, *Ant.* 4.209; Philo, *Prob.* 81–82).
60. This was first noticed by R. Steven Notley, "Jesus' Jewish Hermeneutical Method in the Nazareth Synagogue," in *Early Christianity and Intertextuality*, vol. 2, *Exegetical Studies*, ed. C. A. Evans and H. D. Zacharias, LNTS 392 (London: Continuum, 2009), 46–59.
61. This was first brought to my attention by R. Steven Notley.
62. We have chosen to translate *gemilut hasadim* "deeds of reciprocal kindness" rather than "deeds of loving kindness"—following Gregg Gardener—since, as he argues, the earliest use of this terminology involves an act that is not completely selfless but some response is expected on behalf of the doer. See Gregg Gardener's discussion on translation of *gemilut hasadim* in "From the General to the Specific: A Genealogy of 'Acts of Reciprocal Kindness' (Gemilut Hasadim) in Rabbinic Literature," in *Religious Studies and Rabbinics*, ed. Elizabeth Shanks Alexander and Beth Berkowitz (London: Routledge, 2017).
63. David Flusser, "A New Senstivity in Judaism and the Christian Message" in *Judaism and the Origins of Christianity* (Jerusalem: Magnes Press, 1988), 476; repr. from *HThR* 61/2 (1968):107–127. Flusser draws a connection between this so-called new sensitivity and the statement of Antigonus of Sokho: "Do not be like servants who serve the master [God] on condition of receiving a reward, but [be] like servants who serve the master not on condition of receiving a reward, and let the awe [love] of Heaven be upon you" (470).
64. Flusser, "A New Sensitivity," 474.
65. See Jeffrey P. García, "'What Do I Still Lack?'; idem, "Concerning *tsdqh*: Reexamining the Gospels' Teaching on Charity within the Larger World of Ancient Jewish Halakhah" (forthcoming).
66. The phrase "treasure in heaven," in all three accounts, is again a reference to charity (see also, Matt 6:20; Luke 12:33). This phraseology develops along with the idea that charity is akin to placing some security for oneself with God in heaven. The best exposition on this concept appears in the Tosefta. During the first century there was a famine in Jerusalem; Monobazus, the king of Adiabene (modern day Iraq), a convert to Judaism, decided to open the royal coffers in order to feed the hungry. His family members immediately protested that he had given away their inheritance. To their protests, the king responded: "My ancestors stored treasures for this lower [part], *but I have stored up treasures above… my ancestors stored up treasures where [human] hand can reach, but I have stored up treasures where [human], hand cannot reach*, as it says [in Scripture], righteousness and justice are the foundation of your throne [Psalm 89:14]…. My ancestors stored up treasures in this world, *but I have stored treasures in the world to come*, as it says [in Scripture], And your righteousness shall go before you [Isa. 58:8]…" (*t. Peah* 4:18). The eschatological connection to this passage is evidence for the importance of charity in the Jewish world. It indicates that the giving of alms was of primary importance (Jeffrey P. García, "'Treasure in Heaven': Examining an Ancient Idiom for Charity," in *Jerusalem Perspective*, https://www.jerusalemperspective.com/12036/ [accessed: August 12, 2017]).
67. There is likely no parallel between "slander" and "bearing false witness" since the two infractions, לשון הרע (*t. Peah* 1:2; *t. Avod. Z.* 1:10, 13, 14) and זמם, זוממים, "perjurers," *m. Mak.* 1) are treated differently.
68. García, *Creation, Composition and Condition*, chap. 3.
68. This representation of the triangular relationship belongs to R. Steven Notley.
69. François Bovon, *Luke 3: A Commentary on the Gospel of Luke 19:28–24:53*, Hermeneia (Minneapolis: Fortress Press, 2012), 53–54.
70. Anderson suggests that the initial impetus for this expression derives from a Second Temple interpretation of Prov 10:2, "Treasures gained by wickedness do not profit, but righteousness delivers from death" (Gary Anderson, "A Treasury in Heaven," 351–367); see also idem, *Sin: A History* (Connecticut: Yale University Press, 2012), 180; *Charity: The Place of the Poor in Biblical Tradition* (New Haven: Yale University Press, 2013).
71. In fact, Lev 19:18 and Gen 1:27 are paired together in *Genesis Rabbah*, "Rabbi Akiva said, 'Love your neighbor as yourself" (Leviticus 19:18) is the greatest principle of the Torah, a person should not say since he embarrassed me, I will embarrass him as well…says Rabbi Tanchuman, 'If you do (embarrass your friend back), know before who you are embarrassing—for in the likeness (דמות) of God he made him.'" (24:8). The reworking of Akiva's mishnaic statement brings together two elements that we also find in the Gospels, thereby attesting to the antiquity of this thinking, although we do not find it in other Second Temple sources.
72. Shmuel Safrai, "Naming on the Eighth Day," *Jerusalem Perspective*, https://www.jerusalemperspective.com/2342/ [Accessed: Aug 13th, 2017].
73. Michael Fishbane, *The Haftarot: JPS Bible Commentary* (Philadelphia: JPS, 2002), xxiii.
74. This was brought to my attention by R. Steven Notley.
75. Ben Zion Bokser, "Life and Death," in *Encyclopedia Judaica*, 22 vols. (Farmington Hills: Thomson Gale; Keter Publishing, 2007), 5–6.
76. *Mekhilta de-Rabbi Ishmael*, trans. Jacob Lauterbach, 2 vols., JPS Classic Reissues (Philadelphia: JPS, 2004), 382.
77. This was suggested to me by R. Steven Notley in a private conversation.
78. Shmuel Safrai and Zeev Safrai, *Haggadah of the Sages* (Jerusalem: Carta, 2009), 10–11.